Export Marketing in German

Export Marketing in German

J. M. C. LAWLOR

Intertext Books—Western Language Laboratories Ltd

Published by
International Textbook Company Limited
Kingswood House, Heath & Reach, Leighton Buzzard, Beds. LU7 0AZ
and 450 Edgware Road, London W2 1EG

© J. M. C. Lawlor 1974

All rights reserved. No part of this publication may be reproduced, stored in a retrieval system, or transmitted, in any form or by any means, electronic, mechanical, photocopying, recording or otherwise, now known or hereafter invented, without the prior permission of the copyright owner.

First published 1974

ISBN 0 7002 0245 5

Printed in Great Britain by Galliard (Printers) Ltd, Great Yarmouth

To my wife—*für ihr Verständnis*

Acknowledgements

I should like to thank the following for their help in providing information and/or checking my manuscript:

Herr Werner Popp, Dip. Volkswirt, M.A., Brunn.
Mr George Clare, Managing Director, Axel Springer Publishing Group, London.
Mr Walker of Export Practice Associates, High Wycombe.
Herr W. Wahle, Export Consultant, Evesham.
Herr Breitmar of Schenkers Ltd., London.
Herr Rebholz of M.A.T. Transport Ltd., London
Herr Haumann of the Centralvereinigung Deutscher Handelsvertreter- und Handelsmakler-Verbände (CDH), Cologne.
and
Mrs Kathleen Shaw, translator, Cheltenham, for her painstaking typing and revision of my manuscript.

Contents

	Foreword								xi
	Introduction								xiii
1	Die Anfrage								2
2	Der Preis								8
3	Der Verkauf								16
4	Die Zahlungsbedingungen								24
5	Die Dokumente, die Versicherung und die Einkaufsbedingungen								34
6	Der Transport und die Verpackung								42
7	Der Handelsvertretungsvertrag								54
8	Die Absatzwege								72
9	Die Werbung								84
10	Die Auslandsmarktforschung								98
	Vocabulary—German/English								108
	Vocabulary—English/German								125
	Bibliography								142

Foreword

It is no use for an English businessman who would like to tackle the German market pulling a sour face and making the complaint: 'They don't know my language'. Many of his more successful English competitors will show no sympathy for his self-inflicted injury. They fully realise that, although Germany is a country where English is widely understood, it would be wrong to rely on English as a vehicle of conversation and communication—at least when business is at stake.

I like this book; it is not a manual, reducing the interested reader to boredom with grinding grammar and old-fashioned idioms. It is more like joining an interesting dialogue. A basic knowledge of the German language is, however, required.

I think there are many good and sound arguments for showing at least some interest in the German language. This book is one of them.

Dr Lando Lotter
Head of the Legal Department of the German Chamber of Industry and Commerce in London

Introduction

1. About the Book

The book is intended to serve two purposes. The first is to provide the reader—who is expected to be a businessman with a good working knowledge of conversational German—with the commercial vocabulary he is likely to need whilst conducting a marketing operation in a German-speaking country. The second is to provide a guide to marketing in Federal Germany from a U.K. base. The book can be used in two ways: firstly as a handbook for marketing men in the field and secondly as a textbook for classes in spoken commercial German for advanced students.

Vocabulary, export procedure and marketing information are dealt with in a series of dialogues in German based on an export marketing operation carried out in Federal Germany by a British Company. The subjects covered are shown in the List of Contents on page ix.

Those taking part are the export manager of the company, an agent in Hamburg and the head buyer of a large 'Einkaufszentrale' in Dortmund. There are ten chapters, each containing a dialogue followed by commercial notes with a detailed explanation in English of the subject discussed. The important commercial words are accompanied by a German translation and there is a German/English vocabulary. The dialogues are recorded on cassettes and can be practised by students orally in the language laboratory or on cassette recorders at home. Examples of commercial letters in German are also given in each chapter.

Federal Germany has a population of 61 million and in terms of G.N.P., is the fourth most important country in the world. In terms of the volume of foreign trade—both imports and exports—she takes second place, after the United States. She is our biggest customer in Europe and our second biggest in the world. The German people earn the highest average wages in the E.E.C. They consume over 30 per cent more than their British counterparts.

Sales of British goods have been increasing rapidly since our accession to the Common Market. At the time of writing, however, our share of the German import market is still under 4 per cent. As suppliers we rank sixth, coming after Holland, France, U.S.A., Italy and Belgium. Comparing our exports per head of population of our customer countries, we sell £56 to every Dane, £47 to every Swede, but only £8 to every German. Clearly there is room for improvement of our position.

However, as well as being the biggest and the richest market in Europe, Germany is also the most competitive. German buyers are courted by salesmen from all over the world. They expect to be the target of an aggressive and unremitting sales effort. They rarely respond to unsolicited letters offering a company's products. They believe that if a company has something worth selling they will send someone to sell it. They expect to be visited and to be talked to—in their own language.

German and British businessmen have many things in common: one of them is a preference for speaking their own language. This preference is widely accepted in the case of the British, and English has become established as an international business language. The Germans' preference for their own language is equally strong and as buyers on their own ground they can afford to indulge it. The British businessman must therefore talk to them in their own language if he is to have any hope of lasting success. He must also be prepared to correspond in German, to quote delivery prices in DM and to understand and to use transport, distribution channels and the media as effectively as his competitors. If he fails to do all these things his chances of success in this toughest of all markets are not likely to be great.

The German language is similar in many respects to English, but German is a difficult language to speak correctly. It is full of grammatical pitfalls. No attempt is made in this book to teach grammar as such. It is assumed that those who read it will be familiar with the main grammatical structures of the language. The emphasis is on relevant vocabulary in its proper context. For those with a good general knowledge of the language, learning German commercial vocabulary is not difficult as most long words consist of a group of smaller ones which are already familiar. Examples are 'Lieferzeit', 'Zahlungsweise' and 'unverbindlich'.

German is of course a very useful business language outside the German Federal Republic. It is spoken as a native language in the German Democratic Republic, Switzerland and Austria and as a first or second business language in Czechoslovakia, Hungary, Yugoslavia, Poland and Rumania. It is also useful on occasions in Bulgaria, Holland, Finland, Greece, Sweden, Israel, Iran, Turkey and the U.S.S.R. In many of these countries there are more businessmen who can speak the language than will admit to the fact. Many older men normally avoid using it because of its war-time associations but may be willing to do so if there is no other choice.

A knowledge of conversational and commercial German is likely to increase significantly the effectiveness of British businessmen engaged in marketing not only in the E.E.C., but in many other European countries. It is hoped that this book will help them to acquire it.

2. How to use the Book

2.1 *To the Student*

The purpose of the dialogues at the beginning of each chapter is to provide a live and, it is hoped, interesting context for the subject matter. Some of the vocabulary to be taught is introduced here (in italics) and a list of additional useful words follows. The commercial matters discussed are expanded in the 'commercial notes' referred to by numbers in the text.

If you have the tapes which accompany the book, it is suggested that you play through the first recording of the dialogue without looking at the text. This will familiarise you with the sound of the new words and make them easier to identify and pronounce. It is also good comprehension practice. Having listened to the recording, open the book and read through the text of the dialogue, looking up any words you do not understand in the vocabulary contained in the chapter, or if necessary at the end of the book. Then play the second 'exploded' version of the dialogue with the book open, repeating the phrases.

If you do not have the tapes, read through the dialogue, looking up any words you do not understand in the vocabulary.

From here go on to the commercial notes, which amplify the text. It is suggested you read these right through, as they form a continuous text. If you then read the dialogue again, looking up the commercial notes referred to by the numbers, you will see how each part of the marketing operation mentioned in the text fits into the whole picture.

Finally, read through the vocabulary and memorise as much of it as possible.

2.2 *To the Teacher*

It is hoped that this book will provide a useful source of material for a course in advanced spoken German for businessmen interested in marketing in Western Germany or German-speaking countries.

It is suggested that each lesson is presented by the teacher in the classroom, using the normal technique for audio-lingual material. After a brief explanation in English of the subject being dealt with and a mention of some of the key words (indicated in italics in the text), the first recording of the dialogue is played on a tape recorder.

The students then work through the printed dialogue, translating it if necessary. At this stage only the English translation of the German word should be given. The commercial notes should not be referred to, but the numbers in the text indicate when they apply, and the teacher can sound out the students as to their knowledge of the commercial procedures involved. The notes represent a continuous text and should be dealt with separately as such.

How much time is then devoted to the commercial notes will depend on the level of knowledge of the students and the object of the course.

Most businessmen with experience of exporting will be familiar with the general principles of the subjects dealt with. It should only be necessary to draw their attention to the ways in which these principles are applied in Germany. If, however, the students are not familiar with export procedures, or if they express a particular interest in the details of the subject, time can be devoted to studying these notes in detail. Otherwise they can be used for private study in preparation for post-laboratory work or for reference during actual marketing operations.

After the introductory period, the students can spend about half an hour in the language laboratory (if one is available) listening to the dialogue and repeating the phrases during the second 'exploded' recording. If no laboratory is available, they can listen to the recording several times and repeat the phrases in unison.

The post-laboratory period offers considerable opportunities for expansion of the lesson and for interesting group work, relevant to the business needs of the students. Ideally this session should take place after an interval of at least a day, during which students will have had time to read and absorb the commercial notes and vocabulary. This gap is not, however, essential.

It is suggested that the follow-up session should consist of two parts. First of all there should be some questions on the vocabulary. If possible these should be formulated so as to eliminate the need for English. For example, questions on Chapter 1 could be 'Was sind die Hauptposten eines Angebots?' 'Was schickt man manchmal mit einer Offerte?' (Muster, Zeichnung, Prospekt, u.s.w.).

Following this, it is suggested that students should be given roles to play in situations resembling those of the dialogues. Again, everything should be in German. For example, after the lesson contained in Chapter 2, the scene could be explained as follows:

'Der Exportleiter einer englischen Firma erkundigt sich bei einem Spediteur nach der Lieferung einer Bestellung für 500 Bügeleisen an einen Kunden in Düsseldorf. Er hat seinen ab-Fabrik Preis schon festgestellt und er möchte die zusätlichen Spesen wissen, um einen Preis cif Hamburg zu berechnen.'

To give other students practice, another scene could be as follows:

'Derselbe Exportleiter befindet sich in Düsseldorf und er spricht mit dem Einkaufschef eines Kaufhauses. Das schriftliche Angebot war cif Hamburg. Er berechnet mit dem Kunden einen "Frei Haus" Preis.'

It should be possible for a teacher who has imagination and some knowledge of business transactions (or failing this, who has carefully studied the commercial notes) to invent enough playlets to give all the students a chance to participate. It is very important that they should all have the opportunity of using the new vocabulary. It is only when they have done so that the knowledge will stick. The teacher's description of the scene must include the allotment of specific roles and enough detail to confine discussion to a particular business transaction.

During the conversation, the teacher should take notes, so that mistakes can be pointed out at the end. An alternative is for a tape recording of the conversation to be made. This can be played back and mistakes corrected as they occur. This is a very effective method, but there is not always time for it. If practice in business correspondence is also required, the model letters at the end of each lesson can be used as the basis for letters dictated in German by the teacher or by one student to the others. Their version can then be corrected by the teacher.

Note: Whereas the names and addresses of the organisations given in the Commercial Notes were as far as possible accurate at the time of going to press, the names of the firms and the people referred to in the dialogues are imaginary.

1

Die Anfrage

Das Telefon klingelt...
BAXTER: Hallo!
WITHOF: Ist dort die Firma Mayheat?
BAXTER: Jawohl. Was kann ich für Sie tun?
WITHOF: Ich möchte bitte Herrn Baxter sprechen.
BAXTER: Am Apparat!
WITHOF: Oh, gut! Guten Tag Herr Baxter. Hier Withof. Von der Firma Scheerer Elektro-Geräte in Hamburg. Erinnern Sie sich noch an uns?
BAXTER: Aber natürlich! Guten Tag Herr Withof. Es freut mich von Ihnen zu hören. Womit kann ich Ihnen behilflich sein?
WITHOF: Es ist folgendes, Herr Baxter: wir haben von einer grossen Einkaufsorganisation eine sehr interessante *Anfrage*[1] nach Heizlüftern bekommen. Es handelt sich um die Firma Einkaufring in Dortmund; sie hat ein Angebot für 1.000 Stück verlangt.
BAXTER: Das ist aber höchst interessant! Können Sie mir bitte weitere Angaben machen?
WITHOF: Selbstverständlich. Der *Einkaufschef* hat mir persönlich geschrieben. Er besteht auf höchster Qualität. Die Lüfter müssen äusserst leise laufen, mit einem zuverlässigen Thermostat ausgerüstet sein, und zwei Heizstufen haben: ein tausend Watt und zwei tausend Watt.
BAXTER: Das dürfte kein Problem sein.
WITHOF: Na, hoffentlich werden Sie dasselbe beim *Preis*[1e] sagen! Er soll um DM 30.— liegen.

Mr Baxter, Export Manager of Mayheat Ltd, London, makers of electric fan heaters, has been considering for some time how he can break into the West German market. His firm has received a number of enquiries from German importers and department stores and it appears that its fan heaters are competitive in price and performance. Mr Baxter is in his office when the telephone rings. It is Herr Withof of Scheerer Elektro-Geräte in Hamburg, one of the importers which has been sending them enquiries. Herr Withof gives details of an enquiry he has just received from the central buying office in Dortmund of a large group of department stores. Mr Baxter says that he will fly to Hamburg with the quotation, so that he and Herr Withof can visit the customer together.

BAXTER (*zögernd*): *Ab Werk*,^(1e) natürlich?
WITHOF: Nein, Herr Baxter, *frei Haus!*^(1e)
BAXTER: Um Himmelswillen! Fracht und alles einbegriffen?
WITHOF: Jawohl Herr Baxter. Zoll und Mehrwertsteuer auch.
BAXTER: Das ist aber allerhand. Zu solch einem Preis kann doch niemand verkaufen.
WITHOF: Meinen Sie damit, dass Sie nicht anbieten wollen?
BAXTER: Nein, das habe ich nicht gesagt. Wir müssen uns die Sache erstmal überlegen. Wie steht es mit der *Lieferfrist*?^(1c)
WITHOF: Sie darf 16 Wochen nicht überschreiten. Das heisst: für die ersten einhundert Stück. Danach müssen Teillieferungen von je 300 Stück pro Monat erfolgen.
BAXTER: Das sollte zu machen sein. Noch etwas?
WITHOF: Ja. Wir brauchen Ihre neuesten *Prospekte*,⁽²⁾ auf Deutsch, wenn möglich, und eine *Preisliste*.⁽²⁾ Der Kunde möchte Ihren englischen *Richtpreis* wissen.
BAXTER: So? Ja, gut—wir werden sie Ihnen schicken. Braucht er auch ein *Muster*?⁽²⁾
WITHOF: Das wäre vielleicht zweckmässig. Ja, schicken Sie es uns bitte sobald wie möglich—und per Luftfracht, um Zeit zu gewinnen. Und sorgen Sie bitte dafür, dass die Verpackung^(1d) ausreichend ist—wegen des Schadenrisikos.

BAXTER: Gut, einverstanden. Aber ich überlege gerade, Herr Withof: wäre es nicht vielleicht besser, wenn ich persönlich das Muster und die Offerte nach Deutschland bringen würde? Es handelt sich ja wohl um ein sehr interessantes Geschäft.

WITHOF: Ja, das wäre bestimmt eine bessere Lösung, Herr Baxter. Wir könnten den Kunden zusammen aufsuchen.

BAXTER: Gewiss. Wir könnten zusammen einen 'Frei Haus' Preis errechnen und Sie könnten uns bei der Frage der *Zahlungsbedingungen*[1f] behilflich sein.

WITHOF: Gerne, Herr Baxter. Wann könnten Sie zu uns kommen?

BAXTER: Einen Augenblick, bitte. Ich sehe in meinem Terminkalender nach. Heute ist Mittwoch. . . . Sagen wir: am nächsten Dienstag.

WITHOF: Ja, das passt ausgezeichnet. Wenn Sie mir ein Fernschreiben mit der Nummer Ihres Fluges schicken, hole ich Sie vom Flughafen ab.

BAXTER: Gut. Das ist sehr nett von Ihnen, Herr Withof. Auf Wiedersehen in Hamburg!

WITHOF: Auf Wiedersehen, Herr Baxter!

Vocabulary

ablehnen: to refuse
anbieten: to quote
die Anfrage: enquiry
die Angabe(n): particular(s), detail(s)
das Angebot: offer
das befristete Angebot: offer of limited duration
das freibleibende Angebot: offer subject to alteration
das unverbindliche Angebot: offer without obligation (not binding)
der Auftrag (Aufträge): order(s)
einen Auftrag erteilen: to place an order
einen Auftrag aufgeben: to place an order
der Auftragseingang: receipt of an order
die Auftragserledigung: execution of an order
das Auftragsformular: order form

die Beförderungsart: method of transport
beifügen: to enclose (with letter, etc.)
die Beschaffenheit: nature (of goods)
bestätigen: to confirm
die Bestätigung: confirmation/acknowledgement

bestellen: to order
die Bestellung: order
der Bestellschein: order form
der Bestellzettel: order form
der Betriebsführer: managing director, works manager
der Betriebsleiter: works manager
die Bezeichnung (-en): description(s)
die Broschüre: brochure

der Chef der Einkaufsabteilung: head buyer

der Direktor: director

die Eigenart: characteristic
der Eigentumsvorbehalt: reservation of proprietary rights
einhalten: to keep to (delivery date)
die Einkaufsabteilung: buying department
der Einkaufschef: head buyer
der Erfüllungsort: place of delivery
die Exportabteilung: export department
der Exportleiter: export manager

der Fabrikleiter: works manager
das Festangebot: firm offer

der Gerichtsstand: jurisdiction
der Geschäftsführer: manager
das Gewicht (netto, brutto): weight (net, gross)
die Gültigkeitsdauer: period of validity

die Importlizenz: import licence

der Katalog: catalogue
der Käufer: buyer, customer
der Kunde: customer, client

der Leiter der Einkaufsabteilung: head buyer
der Lieferant: supplier
die Lieferbedingungen: terms of delivery
die Lieferfrist: delivery period
liefern: to supply
der Liefertermin: delivery date
die Lieferung: supply, delivery
die Lieferzeit: time of delivery

der Manager: manager
das Mass: measure
die Menge: quantity, amount
das Muster: sample

der Nachlass (pl. N'lässe): rebate, discount
die Normbezeichnung: standard specification

die Offerte: offer

der Personaldirektor: personnel manager
der Plan: drawing
Preise angeben: to quote prices
ein Preisangebot machen: to submit an offer/a quotation
die Preisliste: price list
das Preisverzeichnis: price list
die Probe: sample
der Produktionsleiter: production manager

die Proformarechnung: proforma invoice
der Prokurist: manager or head clerk (with power to sign binding contracts and to represent the firm in a court of law)
der Prospekt: prospectus

die Qualität: quality
die Quantität: quantity

der Rabatt (pl. Rabatte): rebate, discount

die Skizze: sketch
die Stellung: position, job
die Stückzahl: quantity

die Transportkosten: transport costs

überschreiten: to exceed
die Unterlage: documentation, 'literature'
unverbindlich: not binding

der Verkäufer: salesman
der technische Verkäufer: technical sales representative
der Verkaufsingenieur: sales engineer
der Verkaufsleiter: sales manager
der Verkaufsvertrag: sales contract
die Verpackung: packing
die Verpackungsart: method of packing
die Versandart: method of dispatch
die Versicherung: insurance
der Vertreter: representative, agent
der Vertriebsleiter: marketing manager
verweigern: to refuse
das Verzeichnis: list

die Währung: currency

die Zahlungsbedingungen: conditions of payment
die Zahlungsweise: method of payment
das Zahlungsziel: date or time of payment
die Zeichnung: drawing
der Zoll: customs

Commercial Notes on Enquiries and Quotations

1. A commercial transaction is usually initiated by an enquiry (*Anfrage*) from a customer (*Kunde*) to a supplier (*Lieferant*). The latter prepares a quotation (*Angebot/Offerte*) which usually includes:

(a) A description of the goods (*Bezeichnung der Ware*), their nature (*Beschaffenheit*) and characteristics (*Eigenart*).
(b) Quantity (*Menge/Stückzahl*).
(c) Delivery (*Liefertermin/Lieferfrist/Lieferzeit*).
(d) Terms of Delivery (*Lieferbedingungen*) with details (*Angaben*) of type of packing (*Verpackungsart*), cost of packing (*Verpackungskosten*), method and cost of transport (*Beförderungsart und -kosten*) and insurance (*Versicherung*).
(e) Price (*Preis*) with details of rebates (*Rabatte*) and other reductions (*Nachlässe*). It should be made clear whether the price is ex-works (*ab Werk*) f.o.b. or c.i.f., etc. (see Chapter 2).
(f) Method of payment (*Zahlungsweise*) or terms of payment (*Zahlungsbedingungen*) (see Chapter 4).
(g) Possible remarks (*Vermerke*) concerning proviso on ownership (*Eigentumsvorbehalt*).
(h) Place of delivery (*Erfüllungsort*).
(i) Jurisdiction (*Gerichtsstand*).

2. When required, the quotation will be accompanied by samples (*Muster/Proben*), brochures (*Broschüren/Prospekte*), drawings (*Zeichnungen*), pictures (*Bilder*), and/or price lists (*Preislisten/Preisverzeichnisse*).

The quotation can be firm (*Fest-Angebot*) or valid only for a limited period (*befristetes Angebot*), or it can be 'not binding' (*unverbindliches Angebot*).

If the quotation is accepted (*angenommen*) by the customer, he will place an order (*Auftrag/Bestellung erteilen*). On receipt of the order (*Erhalt*) the supplier should send an acknowledgement (*Auftragsbestätigung*).

Letters concerning Enquiries

1. *Different ways of saying 'we thank you for your letter or enquiry'*

Wir danken Ihnen für Ihr Schreiben vom 30. Oktober.
Wir haben Ihre Anfrage vom 1. November dankend erhalten.
In Beantwortung Ihres Schreibens vom 3. Dezember betreffs Heizlüfter, ...
Für Ihre Anfrage vom 5. Januar danken wir Ihnen bestens.

2. Submitting quotations

We are pleased <u>to quote as follows:</u>
Wir freuen uns Ihnen folgendes anbieten zu können:
<u>Please find enclosed</u> leaflets and price lists.
Wir gestatten uns in der Anlage Prospekte und Preislisten zu überreichen.
We are pleased to submit our quotation.
Es freut uns hiermit unsere Offerte zu unterbreiten.
In reply to your enquiry of 20th February regarding fan heaters, we submit the following quotation:
In Beantwortung Ihrer Anfrage vom 20. Februar, betreffs <u>Heizlüfter</u>, unterbreiten wir Ihnen folgendes Angebot:

3. End of the letter

We should be pleased to let you have any further information which you may require.
<u>Für weitere Auskünfte stehen wir Ihnen gerne zur Verfügung.</u>
Please let us have your order as soon as possible as our stocks are limited.
Wir bitten Sie uns Ihre Bestellung so bald wie möglich <u>zukommen zu lassen,</u> da unsere Vorräte beschränkt sind.
We look forward to hearing from you soon and remain,
Yours faithfully,
Wir sehen Ihrer baldigen Nachricht gern entgegen, Hochachtungsvoll,
In Erwartung Ihrer baldigen Nachrichten empfehlen wir uns Ihnen mit vorzüglicher Hochachtung,

2

Der Preis

WITHOF: Also, Herr Baxter—heute nachmittag haben wir einen Termin bei Herrn Steinemann vom Einkaufring. Er erwartet einen 'Frei Haus'[1.7] Preis von uns. Haben Sie Ihre Offerte bei sich?
BAXTER: Jawohl, Herr Withof, hier ist sie.
WITHOF: Gut. Und wie sind Ihre Preise? F.O.B.?[1.3]
BAXTER: Nein, sie sind C.I.F. Hamburg.
WITHOF: Ach so. Ja, jetzt habe ich's. Also für 1000 Stück ist der Preis DM 24.000.— Es ist gut, dass Sie in unserer Währung anbieten.
BAXTER: Gewiss, aber wir tun es nicht gerne, weil wir das Risiko einer eventuellen Änderung im Wechselkurs tragen müssen. Trotzdem, wir wollen Ihnen soweit wie möglich entgegen kommen.
WITHOF: Gut. Und nun müssen wir den Einfuhrzoll[2.1] berechnen. Wissen Sie vielleicht unter welcher Tarifnummer[2.1] diese Heizlüfter einzuordnen sind?
BAXTER: Ich glaube unter 85–12, 'Elektrische Haushaltsgeräte'.
WITHOF: Ja, das wird wohl stimmen. Das bedeutet einen Zolltarif von 3 Prozent. Drei Prozent von DM 24.000.— ist DM 720.—; also das macht dann insgesamt DM 24.720.— verzollt. Plus Mehrwertsteuer[2.2] von 11%.
BAXTER: Und was für Spesen[2.3] kommen dann noch in Frage?
WITHOF: Das müssen wir mal sehen. Es gibt da mehrere kleine Abgaben und Gebühren,[2.3] wie zum Beispiel Zollmaklergebühren, die Kai-Umschlagsgebühr, das Rollgeld und die Bankspesen. Dazu kommt dann noch der Binnentransport. Sagen wir also einmal insgesamt DM 900.—.
BAXTER: Das wären also DM 25.620.—. Das ist Ihr Einstandspreis.
WITHOF: Stimmt. Aber vergessen Sie bitte nicht, dass dazu noch unser Aufschlag von 25% kommt!
BAXTER: So hoch?
WITHOF: Gewiss, Herr Baxter. Als Handelsvertretung haben wir viele Dienstleistungskosten:[3] Personalkosten, Reisekosten, Postgebühr, Büromaterial und so weiter, und so weiter. . . . Unsere Provision ist keineswegs ein Reinverdienst. Nur ein geringer Anteil davon bleibt als Unternehmergewinn.

Mr Baxter has arrived in Hamburg and is now in Herr Withof's office at Scheerer Elektro-Geräte. Using as a base the C.I.F. price which Mr Baxter has brought with him, they calculate the various amounts, including customs duty, profit and Value Added Tax, which must be added to arrive at a Franco Domicile price.

BAXTER: Ja, ich weiss. Der Kostendruck ist eben sehr stark. Aber wir dürfen den Wettbewerb nicht vergessen.... Trotzdem, sagen wir vorerst einmal 25%. Das macht wieviel ...?

WITHOF: Insgesamt DM 32.025.—, plus 11% *Mehrwertsteuer*. Der *Frei Haus* Preis wäre also DM 35.550.—, rund gerechnet, oder DM 35,55 pro Stück.

BAXTER: Ja, das ist ja nun wesentlich höher als der Preis den Sie ursprünglich erwähnt hatten. Wir werden uns auf unsere überlegene Qualität verlassen müssen.

WITHOF: Oder aber auf Ihre Verkaufsgewandtheit, Herr Baxter!

Vocabulary

die Abgaben (pl.): dues, fees
der Abgangshafen: port of departure
die Änderung: change
der Aufschlag: mark-up
der Aussenstand: outstanding debt
verlorene Aussenstände: bad debts

die Bankspesen: bank charges
benennen (p.p. benannt): to specify, to name
der Betrag: amount
die Betriebsunkosten: overheads
der Binnentransport: inland transport
Brüsseler Zolltarif Schema: Brussels nomenclature
der Bürobedarf: office supplies
die Bürounkosten: office expenses

die Dienstleistungskosten: service costs

der Einfuhrzoll: import duty
der Einkaufspreis: purchase price
der Einstandspreis: cost price
der Einzelhandelspreis: retail price
erheben: to collect levy (tax, etc.)
eventuell: possible

die Fertigungsgemeinkosten: factory overheads
die Fracht: freight
frachtfrei: carriage paid (C.P. or CGE. paid)
Frachtkosten per Nachnahme: carriage forward
frei an Bord/franko Bord: free on board (F.O.B.)
frei Bahnwagen: free on rail (F.O.R.)
frei Güterwagen/Lastkraftwagen: free on truck (F.O.T.)
frei Haus: franco (FCO) domicile
frei Längsseite Schiff: free alongside ship (F.A.S.)
frei Schiff: free on board (F.O.B.)
frei Waggon: free on rail (F.O.R.)

die Gebühr: fee, tax, charge, etc.
die Gesamtsumme: total amount

die Geschäftsunkosten: overheads, business expenses
die Gestehungskosten: production costs
versteuert: duty paid
der Gewichtszoll: specific duty (based on weight)
der Gewinn: profit
die Gewinnspanne: profit margin
der Grundpreis: basic price

der Inlandspreis: home market price

die Kai-Umschlaggebühr: dockside transfer charge
der Kostenaufwand: expenditure
der Kostendruck: pressure of costs
Kosten und Fracht: C. & F. (cost and freight)
Kosten, Versicherung, Fracht: cost, insurance, freight (C.I.F.)

ab Lager: ex-warehouse
der Lastkraftwagen (LKW): lorry
die Lieferbedingungen: terms of delivery
die Lohnkosten: labour costs

die Materialkosten: material costs
die Mehrwertsteuer (M.W.St.): value-added tax (V.A.T.)
der Mengenzoll: specific duty (based on quantity)

der Normalpreis: regular price
der Nutzen: profit, gain

die Personalkosten: salaries, wages
die Position: item
der Posten: item
die Postgebühren: postal charges
der Preis: price
der Preisaufschlag: increase in price, extra charge
die Preiserhöhung: price increase
die Preisermässigung: price reduction
die Preisschwankung: fluctuation in price
die Preisüberwachung: price control
die Preisverordnung: price regulation

der äusserste Preis: lowest price, best possible price
der feste Preis: firm price
der konkurrenzfähige Preis: competitive price
ein mässiger Preis: a reasonable price
der niedrigste Preis: lowest price
einen Preis berechnen, kalkulieren: to arrive at a price, to calculate a price
einen Preis erhöhen, heraufsetzen, steigern: to raise a price
einen Preis ermässigen, herabsetzen, senken: to reduce, lower a price
die Provision: commission

die Raumkosten: cost of premises
der Reinverdienst: nett profit
die Reisekosten: travelling expenses
die Reisespesen: travelling expenses
der Richtpreis: standard price, price recommended by manufacturer but which trade is not obliged to adopt
der Rohgewinnaufschlag: mark-up
das Rollgeld: cartage
die Rollspesen: cartage

der Selbstkostenpreis: cost of production, net cost
die Spesen: expenses
die Stückzahl: quantity
der Stückzoll: specific duty

die Tarifeinordnung: tariff classification
umrechnen: to convert (money)
die allgemeinen Unkosten: general overheads
der Unternehmergewinn: employer's profit
unverzollt: duty unpaid
vereinbaren (einen Preis): to agree (a price)
die Verkaufsgewandtheit: skill in selling
der Verschiffungshafen: port of embarkation
die Verwaltungskosten: administration costs
verzollt: duty paid

der Waggon: railway truck
die Währung: currency
ab Werk: ex-works
der Wertzoll: 'ad valorem' duty

der Zoll: customs duty
zollfrei: duty-free
die Zollmaklergebühren: customs broker's fees
die Zollrückvergütung: repayment of duties paid or 'drawback'
die Zolltarifnummer: customs tariff number

Commercial Notes on Prices and Costs

1. *Transport costs, etc.*

1.1 *Ex works (Ab Werk, Ab Fabrik or Ab Lager)*
The price includes the basic price (Selbstkostenpreis, Grundpreis or Einstandspreis), the general overheads, (allgemeine Unkosten) and the profit (Gewinn). The goods are placed at the buyer's disposal in the seller's factory (Fabrik or Werk) or in his warehouse (Lager). The responsibility of the buyer for freight (Fracht) and insurance (Versicherung) starts when the goods pass the factory gate. Packing (Verpackung) may or may not be included in the price and this is usually specified (e.g. 'Verpackung nicht einbegriffen' or 'einschliesslich Verpackung').

1.2 *F.O.R. (Free on Rail) (Frei Waggon), F.O.T. (Free on Truck) (Frei Lastkraftwagen)*
In this case, the seller puts the goods either on the Railway Authority's vehicles (Lastkraftwagen) or on the railway truck (Waggon). He is responsible for freight and insurance up to that point.

1.3 *F.O.B. (Free on Board) (Frei an Bord)*
The seller is reponsible for the freight and insurance of the goods until they pass over the ship's rail (über die Reling) at a named port of embarkation (Verschiffungshafen). In Germany the English abbreviation F.O.B. is commonly used. (This might also appear as fob or f.o.b.)

1.4 *C. & F. (Cost and Freight) (Kosten und Fracht)*
The seller pays the freight to a named port of arrival (benannter Bestimmungshafen). The insurance is the responsibility of the buyer.

1.5 *C.I.F. (Cost, Insurance, Freight) (Kosten, Versicherung, Fracht)*
The seller has to pay the freight and insurance charges to a named port of arrival (benannter Bestimmungshafen). He is bound to supply the buyer or his agent with a 'Clean Bill of Lading'—B/L—(ein reines Konnossement) and a negotiable Certificate of Insurance (eine übertragbare Seeversicherungspolice). The buyer's responsibilities commence as soon as the goods pass over the ship's rail during unloading at the port of arrival. The English term is usually used, but may also appear in the form of cif or c.i.f.

1.6 *Free Frontier (frei Grenze)*
The seller pays all the charges up to the arrival of the goods at the frontier. The term is used mainly within continental Europe.

1.7 *Franco Domicile or Free delivered (Frei Haus)*
The seller pays all charges up to the delivery of the goods at the buyer's address, including import duty (Einfuhrzoll) and inland cartage (Binnentransport).

2. *Duties and Taxes*

2.1 *Customs duties (Einfuhrzölle)*
These are usually 'ad valorem' (Wertzoll) and are calculated as a percentage of the C.I.F. value. Sometimes they are specific (Gewichts- oder spezifischer Zoll), and are based on nett weight (Nettogewicht), quantity (Stückzahl) or dimensions (Abmessungen) of the goods. Duty is calculated on the basis of Brussels nomenclature (Brüsseler Zolltarif Schema). Duty on British goods going into Germany is on a diminishing scale until it becomes nil in 1977.

2.2 Value-added tax (Mehrwertsteuer)

This is 11% and is charged on the C.I.F. duty-paid price. It has to be paid by the importer, who then charges his customer at the same rate on the uplifted price. On remitting this tax to the Customs Authorities, he deducts the amount already paid. In our case he would have to pay DM 3.530.— less DM 2.719.— which is DM 811.—.

2.3 Calculation of a 'Frei Haus' price

Artikel	Preis DM	Mehrwertsteuer auf 11%
Ware: Heizlüfter		
Menge: 1000 Stck.		
Nettogewicht: 2 Tonnen		
Bruttogewicht: 2,5 Tonnen		
C.I.F.-Wert:	24.000.—	
Zoll auf 3%:	720.—	
Preis C.I.F. Hamburg, verzollt:	24.720.—	2.719.—
Bankspesen, Rollgeld,		
Kai-Umschlaggebühr,		
Aufnehmen auf Lager,		
Binnentransport nach Dortmund	900.—	
Total (Einstandpreis)	25.620.—	
Nutzen: 25%:	6.400.—	
	32.020.—	
Mehrwertsteuer auf 11%:	3.530.—	3.530.—
Total:	35.550.—	

Preis pro Stück: DM 35.55 *Frei Haus, versteuert*, einschliesslich M.W.St.

3. *Commission (Provision), net profit (Reinverdienst) and service costs (Dienstleistungskosten)*

Commission varies considerably from one trade to another. In this case a mark-up (Rohgewinnaufschlag) of 25% will give a profit margin (Gewinnspanne) on the sales price of 20%.

Such high rates of commission are justified by agents on the grounds of constantly rising service costs (Dienstleistungskosten). They tend to rise much more quickly than the cost of the goods they sell.

The charges, which are deducted from the gross profit (Rohgewinn) to arrive at the net profit (Reingewinn) include the following:

personnel expenses	(Personalkosten)
travelling expenses	(Reisekosten)
cost of premises	(Raumkosten)
corporation taxes	(Betriebliche Steuern)
office stationery	(Büromaterial)
depreciation	(Abschreibung)
miscellaneous costs	(Sonstige Kosten)
employer's salary	(Unternehmerlohn)
interest on capital	(Kapitalverzinsung)
car expenses	(Kfz-Kosten)

Letters about the Cost of Shipment and the Price of Goods

1. *Letters to forwarding agents:*
(a) Please let us know the current rates for air-, rail-, road-transport.

Wir bitten um Angabe der derzeitigen Frachtrate für Luft-, Bahn-, Lastwagenversand.

(b) We have an order for dispatch of 100 Fan Heaters from London to Dortmund and should be glad to know your lowest rate.

Wir haben einen Auftrag für den Versand von 100 Heizlüftern von London nach Dortmund und bitten um Ihre niedrigste Fracht-Offerte.

2. *Letters to customers regarding price:*
(a) Our prices are F.O.B. London

Unsere Preise verstehen sich f.o.b. London.

(b) We regret that we cannot supply at the prices shown in your order, which were quoted several months ago. Our best possible price today would be DM 30.— C.I.F. Hamburg.

Wir bedauern, dass wir Ihnen nicht mehr zu dem in Ihrem Auftrag genannten Preis, den wir Ihnen vor mehreren Monaten ~~quotierten~~, liefern können. Unser bestmöglichster Preis wäre heute DM 30.— c.i.f. Hamburg.

(c) As a result of increased labour and material costs we have had to increase our prices by 7%.

Auf Grund ~~steigender~~ *gestiegener* Löhn- und Materialkosten mussten wir unsere Preise um 7% erhöhen.

3

Der Verkauf

BAXTER: Herr Steinemann, es hat uns besonders gefreut, Ihre Anfrage zu bekommen. Bevor wir aber anfangen unser Angebot zu besprechen, darf ich Ihnen einmal kurz ein paar Fragen stellen? Ich möchte mir gerne über Ihre Anforderungen ganz im Klaren sein.
STEINEMANN: Aber natürlich, Herr Baxter.
BAXTER: Danke schön. Meine erste Frage ist die: sind Sie am Gewicht des Heizlüfters interessiert? Soll er möglichst leicht sein?
STEINEMANN: Ja, das soll er wohl. Je leichter, desto besser.
BAXTER: Gut. Zweite Frage: Soll der Heizlüfter auch als Ventilator dienen können?
STEINEMANN: Ja, das wäre gewiss ein grosser Vorteil.
BAXTER: Und er muss äusserst leise laufen, nicht wahr?
STEINEMANN: Ja, Herr Baxter, das ist sehr wichtig. Wir haben eine anspruchsvolle Kundschaft.
BAXTER: Natürlich—versteht sich von selbst! Und nun noch eines: Sie brauchen einen zuverlässigen Thermostat und zwei Heizstufen, 1000 und 2000 Watt, habe ich recht?
STEINEMANN: Stimmt genau. Das steht auf der Anfrage.
BAXTER: Jawohl, ich weiss. Aber ich wollte nur vollkommen sicher gehen, dass wir Ihre Anforderungen genau verstanden haben. Und ich glaube, dass wir genau das richtige Modell haben. Es entspricht Ihren Anforderungen in jeder Hinsicht.
STEINEMANN: Gut. Wann kann ich es mir einmal ansehen?
BAXTER: Ich habe ein Muster mitgebracht. Darf ich es Ihnen gleich zeigen?
STEINEMANN: Bitte, bitte. Aber wir müssen uns etwas beeilen, meine Zeit ist ein bisschen knapp heute.
BAXTER: Ja, natürlich. Ich verstehe vollkommen, Herr Steinemann. Also: kurz gesagt, hier ist der Heizlüfter! Sie können sich selbst von seinen Vorteilen überzeugen.
STEINEMANN: Was für einen Stecker hat er?

Mr Baxter and Herr Withof are now in the office of Herr Steinemann, the Head Buyer of the firm Einkaufring in Dortmund, which sent the original enquiry for the fan heaters.

Mr Baxter makes a planned sales presentation, going through the stages.

D (*Definition*), I (*Identification*), D (*Demonstration*), A (*Acceptance*), D (*Desire*), A (*Action*). He gets the order.

BAXTER: DIN, natürlich, Herr Steinemann. Hier, sehen Sie!
STEINEMANN: Gut. Können wir also einschalten.
Pause. Geräusch des Einsteckens; dann das Einschalten und das Laufen des Apparates.
　Mmmmm.... Nicht schlecht.
Geräusch des Abschaltens.
　Ziemlich leise ist das Gerät ja wohl. Was soll es kosten?
BAXTER: Ihren Wünschen entsprechend haben wir einen Frei-Haus-Preis berechnet. Er beträgt DM 35,55, einschliesslich der Mehrwertsteuer.
STEINEMANN: DM 35,55? Das ist aber sehr teuer, Herr Baxter!
BAXTER: Finden Sie das? Wenn man die Qualität und Leistung in Betracht zieht, glauben wir, dass dieser Preis sehr konkurrenzfähig ist.
STEINEMANN: Das ist Ansichtssache! Sehen Sie hier! Wir verkaufen ein ähnliches Gerät der Firma Gosmet, das Modell MG-03-, für DM 43,50. Mit unserem normalen Gewinn und der Mehrwertsteuer wäre der Einzelhandelspreis Ihres Modells beinahe DM 50,00. Glauben Sie, dass der Kunde ohne Weiteres 15% mehr zahlen würde?
BAXTER: Ja, natürlich, wenn ein Grund dafür besteht. Und Gründe genug gibt es ja wohl. Darf ich gleich zwei nennen? Der geräuschlose Lauf und die Formschönheit. Sie müssen wohl zugeben, dass der Stil besonders elegant ist.
STEINEMANN: Ja, da haben Sie zu einem gewissen Grad recht....
Geräusch des Einschaltens, Laufens, und Abschaltens des Lüfters.
　Geräuscharm ist er auch.... Trotzdem, der Preisunterschied ist beträchtlich. Ich muss mir die Sache erst noch einmal gut überlegen.
BAXTER: Herr Steinemann, ich habe Ihnen nur eines unserer Modelle vorgeführt. Es gibt auch ein anderes, das Ihren Wünschen entsprechen könnte. Hier ist der Prospekt. Wie Sie sehen, es hat keine Ventilationsstufe und der Preis ist DM 5.—, niedriger. Es ist unser Modell HL 250. Gefällt es Ihnen besser?

STEINEMANN: Hmm.... Die Ventilationsstufe ist vielleicht nicht allzu wichtig. ... Ich glaube, dieses Modell ist wirklich besser.
BAXTER: Sie meinen das Modell HL 250? Ja, ich glaube, Sie haben recht. Es könnte wohl ein Verkaufschlager sein. Wieviele solcher Heizlüfter verkaufen Sie normalerweise in einem Jahr?
STEINEMANN: Das kommt auf die Konjunktur an. Etwa 50 000 im Jahr.
BAXTER: Und wenn Sie ein Gerät anbieten, das besondere Vorteile hat...?
STEINEMANN: Na, vielleicht bis zu 70 000 Stück. Bei ganz günstiger Konjunktur!
BAXTER: Und wann verkaufen Sie am meisten? Vermutlich im Spätherbst?
STEINEMANN: Ja, so im Oktober/November.
BAXTER: Das bedeutet, dass Sie die Waren bis spätestens Ende September auf Lager haben müssen, nicht wahr?
STEINEMANN: Nein! Anfang September! Wir müssen reichlich Zeit haben alles zu kontrollieren.
BAXTER: Herr Steinemann: unsere normale Lieferfrist für solche Mengen beträgt 16 Wochen. Das wäre also schon zirka drei Wochen zu spät. Wenn wir aber ausnahmsweise die Frist auf 12 Wochen reduzierten, könnten Sie sich dann schon jetzt entscheiden?
STEINEMANN: Na, könnten Sie das aber fest versprechen?
BAXTER: Jawohl, das kann ich! Nur muss ich unserer Fabrik sofort Bescheid sagen.
STEINEMANN: Ja, also—gut! Unter dieser Bedingung könnten wir es ja wohl einmal probieren. Aber vorläufig sprechen wir noch nicht von 70 000 Stück! Wir werden Ihnen einen Auftrag über 1.000 Stück erteilen. Und wir müssen uns über die Lieferbedingungen ganz und gar im klaren sein!

Vocabulary

abschliessen (Vertrag): to sign a contract
den Anforderungen entsprechen: to meet the requirements
annehmen: to accept (an offer)
um Auskunft bitten: to ask for information

der Bedarf: requirement
benötigen: to need
berechnen: to calculate
beschreiben: to describe
der Beweis: proof
beweisen: to prove, demonstrate
brauchen: to require, to need

die Dauerhaftigkeit: durability
D.I.N. (Deutsches Institut für Normen): German Standards Institute (equivalent to B.S.I.)

sich entscheiden: to decide
erlauben: to allow, permit
erledigen: to settle (business)
erteilen (einen Auftrag): to place an order

ins Geschäft kommen: to do business with
günstig (Angebot): advantageous (offer)

eine günstige Gelegenheit benutzen: to take advantage of an opportunity

sich für etwas interessieren: to be interested in something

der Konkurrent: competitor
die Konkurrenz: competition
konkurrenzfähig: competitive

die Lebensdauer: life, service life

nachkommen: to meet, comply with
nachweisen (einen Vorteil): demonstrate, to prove (an advantage)

passen (jemanden): to fit, to suit (someone)
der Portier: gatekeeper
prüfen: to examine, test
zur Prüfung: on trial

eine bedeutende Rolle spielen: to play an important part

schriftlich bestätigen: to confirm in writing
stören: to disturb
suchen: to look for

die Telefonzelle: telephone box
die Telefonzentrale: telephone exchange

überlegen: to think over
sich überzeugen: to convince oneself

der Verkaufsschlager: good selling line
verlangen: to demand
vorführen: to demonstrate, to show
vorschlagen: to suggest
sich etwas vorstellen: to think of, to imagine
sich jemandem vorstellen: to introduce oneself to someone
der Vorteil: advantage
vorteilhaft: advantageous
den Vorteil ziehen (aus): to take advantage of something

zeigen: to show, to display

Commercial Notes on the Sales Presentation

In this interview with the buyer, Mr Baxter uses a planned sales presentation. This form of approach may be used, with appropriate modifications, for any products, and the stages (Stufen) may be listed as follows:

>Definition (Definition)
>Identification (Identifizierung)
>Demonstration/Proof (Beweis)
>Acceptance (Annahme)
>Desire (Begierde)
>Action/Close (Abschluss)

These stages are described in more detail below, against the notes corresponding to the sentences in the dialogue which begin each one.

1. *Definition* (*Definition*)

    Mr Baxter starts by asking questions which define the exact requirements (Anforderungen) of the customer. He does not open the discussion by describing the product.

2. *Identification (Identifizierung)*
   Having defined the characteristics (Eigenschaften) of the products required by the buyer, Mr Baxter identifies (identifiziert) his own product with them.

3. *Demonstration (Beweis)*
   The demonstration of the product is here linked with the definition. The buyer is encouraged to prove (beweisen) to himself whether the characteristics of the fan heater correspond with those he is looking for.

4. *Acceptance (Annahme)*
   If there had been any doubt as to the customer's acceptance of the suitability of the fan heater, Mr Baxter would have asked him if he had any queries. The customer has, however, clearly been impressed by the heater and his question about the price confirms his interest and acceptance of the sales arguments.

5. *Desire (Begierde)*
   In this case it is not a matter of arousing the personal desire of the buyer for the product, but of convincing him that it will sell well and make a profit. Mr Baxter achieves this by pointing out the reasons why the heater will sell in spite of the higher price.

6. *Action (Abschluss)*
   To close (abschliessen), Mr Baxter first of all uses the technique of offering an alternative. He encourages the buyer to choose between two different models, ignoring the alternative, which is not to buy at all. Finally, he obtains the order by offering a concession on delivery in return for an immediate decision.

Useful Phrases

1. *On the telephone—Making an appointment*
   Kann ich bitte Herrn ... sprechen?
   Darf ich bitte Herrn ... von der Einkaufsabteilung sprechen?
   Ich möchte bitte mit dem Einkaufschef sprechen.
   Könnten Sie mich bitte mit dem Herrn in der Einkaufsabteilung verbinden, der für Heizlüfter zuständig ist?
   Hier spricht Baxter, Exportleiter der Firma Mayheat, Hersteller von Heizlüftern.

Darf ich Sie fragen ob Sie sich im Prinzip für Heizlüfter höchster Qualität interessieren?
Ich möchte Ihnen gerne einen kurzen Besuch machen.
Wenn Sie mir höchstens 15 Minuten widmen wollen, können Sie sich ein Bild davon machen, inwieweit unser Produkt Ihnen nützlich sein könnte.
Passt es Ihnen, wenn ich am ... (Tag) um.... Uhr (Zeit) zu Ihnen komme?
Oder ist es Ihnen am folgenden (an einem anderen) Tag angenehmer?
Mein Anliegen wird höchstens.... Minuten Ihrer Zeit in Anspruch nehmen. Schon nach 5 Minuten können Sie sich entscheiden, ob es Sie interessiert oder nicht.
Kann ich am Montag vielleicht noch einmal anrufen um zu hören, ob es Ihnen möglich ist, mich am Dienstag zu empfangen?
Können wir vorerst Dienstag, etwa um 2 Uhr, festhalten? Falls Ihnen etwas dazwischen kommt, haben Sie vielleicht die Liebenswürdigkeit mich unterrichten zu lassen. Dann brauche ich Sie nicht noch einmal telefonisch zu stören.

2. *At reception* (*beim Empfang*)

   Würden Sie mich bitte bei Herrn Prokurist Schmidt melden?
   Mein Name ist ..., von der Firma ... in ...
   Hier ist meine Besuchskarte.
   Ich bin mit Herrn Schmidt verabredet.
   Ich habe eine Verabredung mit Herrn Schmidt um ... Uhr.
   Der Anlass meines Besuches ist....

3. *Definition and identification stage*

   Darf ich einmal kurz ein paar Fragen bezüglich ... stellen?
   Darf ich gleich zu Anfang eine direkte Frage an Sie richten?
   Sind Sie an ... interessiert?
   Darf ich Sie fragen, ob Sie sich für eine lange Lebensdauer des Produkts interessieren?
   Das ist doch wohl immerhin Ihr Hauptinteresse?
   Haben Sie daran gedacht, dass Sie ... ?
   Suchen Sie eine hohe Leistung?
   Soll ich Ihnen einen Frei Haus Preis anbieten?
   Welche Lieferfrist benötigen Sie?
   Verlangen Sie eine hohe Qualität?
   Spielt die mechanische Festigkeit eine wichtige Rolle?
   Unser Gerät entspricht genau Ihren Anforderungen.

Sicher ist Ihnen bekannt, dass. . . .
Legen Sie Wert auf . . . ?
Passt Ihnen diese . . . ?
Wäre es ein Vorteil wenn . . . ?
Dieses Modell ist wohl am zweckmässigsten.

4. *Demonstration and acceptance stages*

Darf ich Ihnen erklären, wie Sie. . . .
Jetzt können Sie sich davon überzeugen.
Finden Sie nicht?
Habe ich mich einigermassen klar ausgedrückt?
Haben Sie sich davon überzeugt, dass dieses Gerät wirklich robust ist?
(. . ., wie robust dieses Gerät ist?)
Sind Sie sich darüber im Klaren?
Dann könnte man also davon ausgehen, dass sie um so mehr einbringt, je eher Sie sie benutzen.
Es lohnt sich also für Sie.
(To a retailer):
Wie wäre es, 500 dieser Geräte pro Monat zu verkaufen?

5. *Action stage*

Was würden Sie sagen, wenn der Preis 10% niedriger wäre?
Wenn Sie sich sofort entscheiden, werden wir gegen Ende des Monats liefern können.
Welches Modell ziehen Sie vor, das Grosse oder das Kleine?
Welches Modell gefällt Ihnen besser?
Nehmen Sie die Gelegenheit wahr, denn noch können wir innerhalb eines Monats liefern.
Wieviele . . . brauchen Sie innerhalb eines Jahres?
Könnten Sie mir eine Idee von Ihrem Jahresbedarf geben?
Sollen wir 600 oder 800 Stück schicken?
Wollen Sie 800 haben, oder reichen es vorerst 500?
Dann wäre es wohl zweckmässig, das Modell so bald wie möglich auszustellen, nicht wahr?
Falls wir ein kleineres Modell anbieten könnten, würde das Gerät dann Ihren Wünschen entsprechen?
Welche Änderungen möchten Sie haben, damit es (das Modell) Ihren Anforderungen genügt?
Wir sind bereit, ein Zahlungsziel von 6 Monaten einzuräumen. Wären Sie damit zufrieden?

Sind Sie sich möglicherweise noch über einiges im Unklaren?
Sie sind noch nicht ganz überzeugt, nicht wahr?
Ist das der Grund, der Sie davon abhält, sich jetzt zu entscheiden?

Letters about Orders received

(a) Thank you for your order No. 8654, for which we enclose our official confirmation.

Wir danken Ihnen für Ihren Auftrag Nr. 8654 und fügen unsere formelle Bestätigung bei.

(b) We thank you for your order No. 8912, dated 3rd March for 100 fan heaters.

Wir bestätigen hiermit dankend Ihren Auftrag Nr. 8912 vom 3. März, *über* ~~für~~ 100 Heizlüfter.

(c) Your instructions have been carefully noted and we hope to have the goods ready for dispatch by the 4th of April.

Wir haben von Ihren Anweisungen Kenntnis genommen und hoffen Ihre Bestellung spätestens am 4. April ~~sendebereit~~ *versandbereit* zu haben.

(d) We very much regret that we have been unable to complete your order by the 4th of April.

Zu unserem grossen Bedauern ist es uns leider nicht möglich gewesen Ihrer Bestellung vor dem 4. April nachzukommen.

(e) The delay is due to a strike/shortage of raw materials/circumstances beyond our control.

Infolge eines Streiks/mangelnder Rohstoffe/unvorhergesehener Umstände konnten wir den gegebenen Liefertermin leider nicht einhalten.

4

Die Zahlungsbedingungen

STEINEMANN: Also, wie gesagt, Herr Baxter: sprechen wir von den Lieferbedingungen.
BAXTER: Gerne, Herr Steinemann. Was möchten Sie wissen?
STEINEMANN: Zunächst die Zahlungsbedingungen. Wie sind die normalerweise?
BAXTER: Ehrlich gesagt, Herr Steinemann, wir haben bis jetzt nur wenig Erfahrung im deutschen Markt. Auf anderen ausländischen Märkten ist unsere Firma immer sehr vorsichtig gewesen. Wir könnten aber kaum in diesem Fall von *Vorauszahlung*[(1)] sprechen. Wie wäre es mit einem *Akkreditiv?*[(2)]
STEINEMANN: Kommt nicht in Frage!
BAXTER: Eine Sichttratte, vielleicht?
STEINEMANN: Wir sind an einen vierteljährlichen Rechnungsabschluss gewöhnt.
BAXTER: Ich bedaure sehr, Herr Steinemann, aber eine solche Zahlungsfrist wäre ausgeschlossen. Bei uns herrscht Kreditknappheit! Und die Zinsen sind sehr hoch! Könnten wir nicht einen *Sichtwechsel*[(3.1)] auf Sie ziehen?
STEINEMANN: Ein *Zeitwechsel*[(3.1)] wäre besser!
BAXTER: Ein *30-Tage Wechsel?*[(3.1)]
STEINEMANN: Wenn Sie darauf bestehen....
BAXTER: Ja, das muss ich leider.
STEINEMANN: Also gut! Und Sie werden uns natürlich in DM in Rechnung stellen, nicht wahr?
BAXTER: Ja, machen wir.
STEINEMANN: Und wie ist es bei grösseren Stückzahlen? Bekommen wir einen *Mengenrabatt?*[(4)]
BAXTER: Ja, gewiss. Für Bestellungen mit einem Wert von mehr als DM 350.000 gewähren wir einen Rabatt von 5%.
STEINEMANN: Gut. Und wenn wir prompt zahlen? Gibt es ein *Skonto?*[(4)]
BAXTER: Das kommt darauf an.... Aber wenn Sie weitere Aufträge erteilen, wird das Geschäft voraussichtlich über die Firma Scheerer laufen. Sie wird Ihnen sicher ein Skonto für *Promptzahlung* gewähren. Mit dieser Firma würden Sie vermutlich in *laufender Rechnung*[(3.2)] stehen.

Mr Baxter discusses with Herr Steinemann, the Head Buyer, alternative terms of payment. These include open account, sight draft and a 30-day draft. They also talk about quantity discounts and rebates.

STEINEMANN: Ja, das ist wohl anzunehmen.
BAXTER: Die Firma ist ein erfahrener Importeur. Sie wird sich um alle Importformalitäten kümmern.
STEINEMANN: Gut. Das wird für uns einfacher sein. Aber für diesen Auftrag hier stehen wir in direkter Verbindung, nicht wahr? Könnten wir bitte kurz über die Dokumente sprechen, die wir von Ihnen zu erwarten haben? Und auch über unsere Einkaufsbedingungen!

Vocabulary

das Akkreditiv: letter of credit
akzeptieren: to accept
die Anzahlung: deposit

die (Bank) Überweisung: (bank) transfer
das Bargeschäft: cash transaction
barzahlen: to pay cash
die Barzahlung: cash payment
begleichen: to pay (a debt)
bestätigen: to confirm
bestätigt: confirmed (as L/C.)
die Bestätigung: confirmation

der Debitsaldo: balance payable
diskontieren: to discount
das Dokumentenakkreditiv: documentary letter of credit
die Dokumententratte: documentary draft
Dokumente gegen Wechselakzept: documents against acceptance (D/A)
Dokumente gegen Zahlung: documents against payment (D/P)

der Eigentumsvorbehalt: reservation of proprietary rights
die Einziehung von Schulden: debt collecting
eröffnen: to open (an account, a letter of credit)

fällig werden: to become due, to mature (a bill)
die Fälligkeit: maturity (of bill)
bei Fälligkeit: at maturity
die Frist: time limit (for payment, etc.)

gültig: valid
zu Gunsten: in favour of
der Guthabensaldo: credit balance

der Importeur: importer

Kasse gegen Dokumente: cash against documents (C.A.D.)
der Kontoauszug: statement

auf ein Konto einzahlen: to pay into an account
der Kursstand: rate of exchange

bei Lieferung zahlen: cash on delivery (C.O.D.)
der Liefertermin: delivery date

der Monatsabschluss: monthly settlement
die Monatsberechnung: monthly account

gegen Nachnahme: C.O.D.
unter Nachnahme: C.O.D.

die Pauschalzahlung: lump sum payment
der Postscheck: postal cheque
präsentieren: to present (a bill, etc.)
die Proformarechnung: proforma invoice
die Promptzahlung: prompt payment

das Quartal: quarter (three months)
die Quartalsabrechnung: quarterly statement of account
die Quartalsrechnung: quarterly bill
die Quartalszahlung: quarterly payment
quittieren (eine Rechnung): to receipt an invoice
die Quittung: receipt

die Rate: instalment
die Ratenzahlung: payment by instalments
die Rechnung: bill, account
der Rechnungsbetrag: total amount
laufende Rechnung: open account
in laufender Rechnung stehen: to have an open account
offene Rechnung: open account
der vierteljährliche Rechnungsabschluss: quarterly credit
der Restbetrag: balance

der Saldo: balance
der Scheck: cheque
die Sichttratte: sight or demand draft or bill

der Sichtwechsel: sight or demand draft (DD).

der Teilbetrag: instalment
die Teilzahlung: instalment
die Tratte: draft

unbestätigt: unconfirmed
unwiderruflich: irrevocable

die Vorauszahlung: payment in advance/ before dispatch
vorlegen: to present (a bill, etc.)

die Währung: currency
das Währungsrisiko: exchange risks
die Währungsschwankung: exchange fluctuation
der Wechsel: bill of exchange (B/E)
einen Wechsel ziehen (auf jemanden): to draw a bill of exchange (on someone)
widerruflich: revocable
der Wortlaut: wording (terms of contract)
der 30-Tage Wechsel: 30-day bill

zahlbar bei Auftragserteilung: cash with order
zahlen: to pay
die Zahlung: payment
die Zahlung auf Ziel: payment on credit terms
Zahlung leisten: to make payment
die Zahlung bei Eingang der Waren: payment on receipt of goods
die Zahlungsbedingungen: conditions of payment
die Zahlungsfrist: term of payment (in time, not method)
die Zahlungsmodalität: method of payment
der Zahlungstermin: day of payment or of maturity (B/E)
die Zahlungsüberweisung: remittance, bank transfer
das Zahlungsversprechen: promissary note
das Zahlungsziel: period of payment
der Zeitwechsel: time bill
gegen 3 Monate Ziel: against 3 months credit
auf Ziel (Zahlung): on credit
30 Tage netto: 30 days net

Commercial Notes on Terms of Payment

Debt collection (Einziehung von Schulden) in a foreign country, even within the E.E.C., is more difficult than at home and there are also risks (Risiken) associated with rates of exchange (Kursstände) and, more rarely, currency restrictions (Devisenbeschränkungen). There are several ways of arranging payment so that one can reduce these risks to a minimum. They can be divided conveniently into three groups: payment before delivery (Vorauszahlung), payment at the time of delivery (Zahlung zur Zeit der Lieferung) and payment after delivery (Zahlung nach der Lieferung).

It should be noted that the Germans, unlike the French and the Italians, do not habitually use bills of exchange (Wechsel). They prefer to deal on open account terms (in laufender Rechnung stehen). They may even feel slightly insulted if it is suggested that a letter of credit or a bill of exchange should be used. However, it may be necessary to use these methods of payment on occasion, so they have been included in this chapter. Usually, however, it would be better to take out a banker's reference (Bankauskunft) on the firm and deal on open account terms.

1. *Payment before delivery* (*Vorauszahlung*)

   From the exporter's point of view this is clearly the safest possible method of payment. It is normally made with the order (bei Bestellung), against a pro-forma invoice (gegen Proformarechnung). The payment is made by bank transfer (Banküberweisung). Instead of paying the full amount, the buyer (Käufer) can pay a deposit or a payment on account (Anzahlung).

2. *Payment at the time of delivery* (*Zahlung zur Zeit der Lieferung*)

   This can be arranged by means of a letter of credit (Akkreditiv). This is a contract (Vertrag) whereby a bank undertakes to pay on behalf of a foreign buyer (ausländischer Käufer) the cost of goods against delivery of the documents which represent them (gegen Vorlage der Dokumente, welche die Ware repräsentieren). The buyer instructs his banker to open a letter of credit in favour of the seller (Verkäufer) for the amount due. When the goods are shipped, the seller presents the documents to the bank and receives payment. These documents (Dokumente) usually consist of the bill of lading (Konnossement) and the commercial invoice (Handelsrechnung), together with other documents as specified.

   The credit can be either revocable (widerruflich), in which case the importer or his banker may cancel or modify it (es annulieren oder abändern), or it can be irrevocable (unwiderruflich), in which case it can only be cancelled or modified with the agreement of all parties involved, i.e. importer, bank and exporter. The credit can also be either unconfirmed (unbestätigt) or confirmed (bestätigt). In the former case the paying bank, usually a correspondent of the importer's bank (Korrespondenzbank) in the exporter's country, is under no contractual obligation towards the exporter. Its obligation to pay is the same as that of the importer's own bank, but no greater. If, however, the credit is confirmed by the paying bank in the exporter's country, this bank is contractually bound (vertraglich verpflichtet) towards the exporter. The exporter has a double guarantee (zweifache Garantie): he has the guarantee of the overseas bank (Überseebank) and the guarantee of the bank in his own country.

   A letter of credit can be payable on presentation of the documents (gegen Vorlage der Dokumente) or at a later date (zu einem späteren Zeitpunkt) against an accepted bill of exchange (gegen Wechselakzept).

   A sample letter of credit is shown in Note 5.2.

3. Payment after delivery (*Zahlung nach Lieferung*)

In spite of the increased risks (Risiken) run by the exporter, this is the most commonly used method of payment. There are various ways in which it can be effected:

3.1 By bill of exchange (*Wechsel or Tratte*)

The documentary bill or draft (Dokumentenwechsel) is the safest for the exporter. The documents of title to the goods (Rechtstitel) are attached to the draft and sent by the exporter's bank to the correspondent in the buyer's country. The documents are only handed over to the buyer on his signing of the draft.

The draft may be a sight draft (Sichtwechsel), which means payment is due immediately after it is presented. This transaction is known as 'documents against payment' (DP.) (Zahlung gegen Dokumente) or, if no draft is used, it is known as 'cash against documents' (C.a.D.), (Kasse gegen Dokumente).

It may also be a time draft (Nachsichttratte/Zeitwechsel) and in this case the buyer receives the documents in return for accepting the draft. He signs it and writes 'accepted' (akzeptiert) on it and it is then payable on maturity (bei Fälligkeit). This is known as 'documents against acceptance' (Dokumente gegen Wechselakzept), the English abbreviation being d/a or D/A.

A bill of exchange may be sent to the buyer for acceptance independently of the document of title. In practice this has to be done if no 'bill of lading', giving title to the goods, is used. The bill is returned by the buyer to the seller, who may discount it (diskontieren) with a bank or present it for payment on maturity (Fälligkeit).

3.2 Open Account (*laufende Rechnung*)

Under these terms the buyer pays by bank transfer (Banküberweisung). This might be on arrival of the goods (bei Eingang der Waren) or on arrival of the invoice (bei Erhalt der Rechnung). More often the buyer pays after a period of credit (auf Ziel). Examples of such terms are: monthly settlement (Monatsabschluss), 30 days net (30 Tage netto), payment within 30 days of Invoice (Zahlung innerhalb von 30 Tagen nach Rechnungsdatum) and quarterly credit (vierteljährlicher Rechnungsabschluss).

4. Skonto

'Ein Skonto' is a discount. It is usually used in connection with prompt payment.

4.1 Rabatt

'*Ein Rabatt*' is a rebate or discount, and it usually depends on quantities ordered—a quantity discount (Mengenrabatt).

5. Letters of Credit

5.1 Letter of Credit (*English*)

By order of ....

for account of ....

we open irrevocable/revocable documentary credit No. ....

in favour of ....

for a sum of .... maximum/about

available at sight/by draft at .... on you

against draft at sight/at .... on ....

against / accompanied by the following documents ....

covering .... (goods) part shipments permitted/prohibited.

Credit valid until .... for presentation for payment/accept. / negotiation

with your ....

Please advise .... by cable/mail of the opening of this credit

without adding / adding your confirmation.

Method of reimbursement: Documents to be sent to ....

5.2 Akkreditiv (Deutsch)

Auftrags ....

für Rechnung ....

eröffnen wir ein unwiderrufliches/widerrufliches Dokumenten-Akkreditiv

No. .... zu Gunsten ....

über höchstens/ca. ....

benutzbar bei Sicht/durch .... Tage-Tratte auf Sie ....

benutzbar gegen Sichttratte .... Tage-Tratte auf ....

begleitet von / gegen folgende(n) Dokumente(n): ....

über .... (Waren)
Teilverschiffungen erlaubt/nicht gestattet.

Dieses Akkreditiv ist gültig bis .... zur Vorlage zwecks Zahlung/Akzeptierung
Negoziierung

bei Ihrer ....

Bitte benachrichtigen Sie .... durch Kabel/Briefpost von der Eröffnung dieses Akkreditivs ohne/unter Beifügung Ihrer Bestätigung.

Remboursanweisung: Die Dokumente sind zu senden an ....

Letters about Terms of Payment

(a) Our usual terms are cash against documents.
    Unsere üblichen Zahlungsbedingungen sind Kasse gegen Dokumente.
(b) We should like payment by confirmed irrevocable letter of credit.
    Wir erbitten Zahlung gegen unwiderruflich bestätigtes Akkreditiv.

(c) For orders of 1000 and over we shall be able to allow a special discount of 5%.

Bei Bestellungen von wenigstens 1000 Stück gewähren wir einen Sonderrabatt von 5%.

(d) This offer is firm for 28 days.

Dieses Angebot ist fest für 28 Tage.

(e) We enclose a Pro-forma invoice in duplicate.

Wir fügen unsere Proformarechnung in doppelter Ausführung bei.

5

Die Dokumente, die Versicherung und die Einkaufsbedingungen

STEINEMANN: Also—die Dokumente. Sie werden uns natürlich Ihre Handelsrechnung[1.1] schicken. Aber vergessen Sie bitte nicht, dass wir drei Exemplare davon brauchen.

BAXTER: Ich notiere das... drei Exemplare. Und wir senden Ihnen auch eine Versandanzeige[1.6] mit den Waren.

STEINEMANN: Und eine mit separater Post, bitte—am Tag des Versands.

BAXTER: Gerne, Herr Steinemann.

STEINEMANN: Wenn Sie C.I.F. liefern, brauchen wir auch ein 'T'-Formular,[1.2] um aus dem E.W.G. Zolltarif Nutzen zu ziehen. Das ist ein T2, nicht wahr?

BAXTER: Nein, während der Übergangszeit verwenden wir ein T3L-Formular. Erst ab August 1977 werden wir das T2-Formular verwenden. Aber wir liefern 'Frei Haus'. Sie brauchen sich nicht darum zu kümmern.

STEINEMANN: Ach ja, das hatte ich vergessen. Könnten Sie uns aber bitte ein Exemplar der Versandbescheinigung[1.3] schicken? Es könnte sein, dass wir es als Nachweis für einen Versicherungsanspruch brauchen. Erst vorige Woche hatten wir einen solchen Fall.

BAXTER: Wenn Sie einen Versicherungsanspruch erheben wollen, schicken wir Ihnen gerne eine Kopie der Versandbescheinigung. Übrigens, was für eine Versicherung[2] möchten Sie—F.P.A.?

STEINEMANN: F.P.A.? Was heisst das? Oh ja! Ich weiss: Sie meinen ohne Particular-Havarie. Nein danke. Ich glaube eine 'all risks' Versicherung wäre besser. Es handelt sich hier um empfindliche Geräte.

BAXTER: Da haben Sie allerdings Recht. Eine 'all risks' Versicherung wäre viel besser. Wir haben eine laufende Police und können Ihnen für jede Lieferung ein Versicherungszertifikat schicken.

Mr Baxter continues his discussion with Herr Steinemann, the Head Buyer. They talk about the documents which will be required under the C.I.F. contract. They discuss the insurance to be effected and the conditions of purchase set out on the back of the order form.

STEINEMANN: Gut, geht in Ordnung. Und jetzt wollen wir einmal unsere *Einkaufsbedingungen*⁽³⁾ anschauen. Sie stehen hier—auf der Rückseite unseres Auftragsformulars.

BAXTER: Ja, gerne, Herr Steinemann.

STEINEMANN: Da ist zuerst die Frage der *Garantie*. Wie lange dauert sie?

BAXTER: Ein Jahr.

STEINEMANN: Gut. Und Sie werden Geräte, bei denen irgendwelche Mängel festzustellen sind, kostenlos ersetzen?

BAXTER: Selbstverständlich. Vorausgesetzt natürlich, dass das Gerät nicht unsachgemäss behandelt wurde.

STEINEMANN: Das versteht sich von selbst, Herr Baxter. Und was für einen *Kundendienst* bieten Sie?

BAXTER: Unsere hiesige Vertretung, die Firma Scheerer Elektro Geräte, hat einen 48-Stunden Reparatur-Service.

STEINEMANN: Gut. Das ist heutzutage wirklich unentbehrlich. Dieser Abschnitt ist sehr wichtig: 'Nichteinhaltung der vereinbarten Lieferfristen und Termine berechtigt uns, ohne Inverzug- und Nachfristensetzung vom Vertrag zurückzutreten und Schadenersatz wegen Nichterfüllung zu verlangen.'

BAXTER: Ja, ich verstehe, Herr Steinemann. Es könnte aber natürlich *höhere Gewalt* vorkommen.

STEINEMANN: Ja, aber sehen Sie hier: 'Höhere Gewalt entlastet den Lieferanten nur, wenn er die Umstände welche sie begründen sollten, uns so rechtzeitig mitteilt als er dazu in der Lage ist.'

BAXTER: Ja, gut. Das ist also klar.

STEINEMANN: Und nun noch der *Gerichtsstand*. Der ist natürlich Dortmund. Und das *Recht* der Bundesrepublik Deutschland gilt ausschliesslich—wenn es jemals dazu kommen sollte. . . .
BAXTER: Herr Steinemann, ich bin überzeugt davon, dass es soweit niemals kommen wird!

Vocabulary

das Abhandenkommen: loss (being mislaid)
abschliessen (eine Versicherung): to effect an insurance
abziehen: to deduct from payment
die Ausfertigung: copy (of B/L., etc.)
die Ausfuhrbewilligung: export licence
die Ausführung: workmanship, design, construction, execution
aushändigen: to hand over (B/L., etc.)

der Beförderungsvertrag: contract of carriage
beglaubigen: to certify
die Beglaubigung: certification
berichtigen: to rectify, to correct
das Billigkeitsrecht: law of equity
der Binnentarif: intra E.E.C. tariff

die Devisenkontrolle: exchange control
das Durchkonnossement: 'through' bill of lading

die Eigentumsübertragung: transfer of ownership
einbehalten: to deduct (from payment)
die Einfuhrbewilligung: import licence
die Einfuhrgenehmigung: import licence
die Einfuhrlizenz: import licence
einsetzen: to appoint
die Einzelpolice: single policy
die Empfangsbestätigung: acknowledgement of receipt
entschädigen: to indemnify
der Entwurf: design
erleiden (Schaden): to suffer (damage or loss)
erwerben (Versicherungspolice): to take out (insurance policy)
E.W.G.: E.E.C.

fehlerhaft: faulty, defective, deficient
das Formular: the form
die Fracht: cargo, freight
der Frachtbrief: consignment note, way bill
Frei von Beschädigung ausser im Strandungsfall: F.P.A. policy (free of particular average)
Frei von Beschädigung wenn unter 3%: W.P.A. policy (with particular average)
die Frist: time limit, date, deadline
der Fristablauf: deadline, expiration of a period
die Frist einhalten: to meet the deadline

die Garantie: guarantee
garantieren: to guarantee
gedeckt sein: to be held covered
die Generalpolice: 'open' policy
das Gericht: court of law
der Gerichtsstand: jurisdiction
der Gesamtwert: total value
die Gewährleistung: warranty, guarantee
die höhere Gewalt: 'force majeure'

haften: to be held liable
die Haftung: liability
die Handelsrechnung: commercial invoice
die Havarie: average, damage (by sea)
die grosse (gemeinschaftliche) Havarie: G.A. (general average)
die kleine Havarie: particular average

indossieren: to endorse
die Inverzugsetzung: warning, unconditional request for performance

die Klausel: clause
das Konossement (rein): (clean) bill of lading
die Konsulatfaktura: consular invoice
das Kontingent: quota

die Lage: status, situation
liberalisieren: to liberalize
die Lieferfrist: delivery time
der Lieferschein: delivery note
der Luftfrachtbrief: airway bill

der Mangel: defect
das Material: material

die Nachfristsetzung: extension of time (granted to debtor, etc.)

die Pauschalpolice: 'flat rate' policy
die Police: policy
die laufende Police: 'declaration', 'open' or 'floating' policy
die Prämie: premium

rechtskräftig sein: to have the force of law
die Reederei: shipper (shipping company)
das Risiko: risk

der Schaden (pl. Schäden): damage, defect
der Schadenersatz: compensation
schadenersatzpflichtig: liable to pay damages
der Schiedsrichter: arbitrator
der Schiedsspruch: arbitration
die Schiffsladung: cargo
der Schiffszusammenstoss: collision at sea
die Schlichtung: conciliation
die Spediteurübernahmebescheinigung: certificate of shipment
die Strafklausel: penalty clause
die Strandung: stranding, shipwreck
im Strandungsfall: in case of shipwreck
der Streik: strike
der wilde Streik: wildcat strike
der Streit: the dispute

einen Streit durch Schiedsspruch erledigen: to settle a dispute by arbitration

die Taxe: valuation, assessment
der Termin: deadline
das Transportdokument: shipping document

die Übergangszeit: transition period
übertragbar: negotiable, transferable
das Ursprungszeugnis: certificate of origin

das Verbrennen: burning
der Verlust: loss
die Versandanzeige: dispatch note
die Versandbescheinigung: certificate of shipment
die Versandpapiere: shipping documents
die Verschollenheit: disappearance
das Versenken: sinking
der Versicherer: insurer/underwriter
der Versicherte: insured
die 'all risks' Versicherung: 'all risks' insurance
die Versicherung mit Havarie: W.P.A. policy
die Versicherung ohne Particular Havarie: F.P.A. policy
der Versicherungsagent: insurance agent
die Versicherungsdeckungsnote: insurance cover note
der Versicherungsmakler: insurance broker
die Versicherungsgesellschaft: insurance company
die Versicherungspolice: insurance policy
das Versicherungszertifikat: insurance certificate
die Verspätung: delay
die Vertragsstrafe: penalty

die Warenverkehrsbescheinigung: movement certificate
der Wohnsitz: domicile

die Zeitpolice: 'floating', 'declaration' or 'open' policy

Commercial Notes on Documentation, Insurance and Terms of Purchase

This chapter deals with those export documents which are likely to be of interest to the buyer. The first part describes the documents which may have to be provided by the seller when the goods are dispatched. The second part deals with types of insurance and the third with the conditions of purchase. The latter are in practice usually superseded (ersetzt) by the seller's terms of sale, contained on the back of his order-acknowledgment. But some buyers may insist on their own terms being observed.

1. *The principal documents to be supplied by the seller include:*

1.1 *The commercial invoice (Handelsrechnung)*
This is an essential part (wesentlicher Bestandteil) of the documentation (Dokumentensatz). It not only shows the debt (Schuld) between the buyer and the seller, but it also serves as evidence (Beläg) for import duty and VAT (Einfuhrzoll und Mehrwertsteuer) as well as for currency control (Devisenkontrolle). It should show at least the description of the goods (Bezeichnung der Ware), the price (Preis), the quantity (Menge), method of dispatch (Versandsart) and the number and marking of the packages (Anzahl und Markierung der Frachtstücke).

1.2 *The movement certificate (Warenverkehrsbescheinigung)*
Under the E.E.C. Community Transit System (C.T.) a movement certificate is used to provide evidence that the goods concerned are in free circulation (freier Verkehr). The 'T-form'-system is used by member states—form T3L by newly-joined members such as the U.K. during the transition period (Übergangszeit)* and form T2 by the six original member states. These forms are status (Lage) cum transit (Transit) documents. They are used to support any customs entry (Zolldeklaration) made for the goods when entitlement to free entry (zollfreier Einfuhr) or payment of duty at the intra-community rate (E.W.G. Binnentarif) is claimed.
When goods are shipped from the U.K. to the old E.F.T.A. countries the movement certificate takes the place of the old certificate of origin (Ursprungszeugnis). Special forms are used, for example form AOS.1 for Austria, ACH.1 for Switzerland and AS.1 for Sweden.

1.3 *The certificate of shipment (Versandbescheinigung)*
This is a document issued by the carrier (Spediteur) to the consignor, certifying that the goods have been received for shipment. It may be required by the buyer to support a claim for loss or damage.

* up to 1.7.1977.

1.4 *The consignment note (Frachtbrief)*
This is a document issued by transport companies and completed by the consignor with his instructions for forwarding the goods. Railway companies issue a rail consignment note (Bahnfrachtbrief), and airlines an air consignment note (Luftfrachtbrief). It is used for goods sent both as separate items and as groupage (Sammelverkehr).

1.5 *The bill of lading (Konnossement)*
This is the principal document in a C.I.F. contract for goods sent by sea. It is an acknowledgement of receipt (Empfangsbestätigung) of the goods by the shipping company (Schiffahrtsgesellschaft), a contract of carriage (Beförderungsvertrag) and a document of title (Inhaberpapier).
It is negotiable (übertragbar) and represents the goods themselves as far as ownership is concerned. Its use makes it possible to delay transfer of the title to the goods until payment has been assured. However, in view of the delays involved and the fact that few goods going to Europe are shipped separately, its use is somewhat restricted.

1.6 *The dispatch note (Versandanzeige)*
This is sent with the goods, giving details of the contents of each package, but not the price. A copy may be sent by separate post to the consignee.

Other documents which may be required, but which are not often used for European destinations include the consular invoice (Konsulat Factura), certificate of origin (Ursprungszeugnis) export licence (Ausfuhrlizens) and import licence (Einfuhrlizens or Einfuhrbewilligung). The latter are only required if quotas (Kontingente) are in force for the goods in question.

2. *The insurance policy (Versicherungspolice)*
The policy taken out by the seller to insure goods in transit against loss or damage (Verlust oder Schaden) may be either a single policy (Einzelpolice) or a declaration policy, known also as a 'floating' or 'open' policy (general Police, laufende Police oder Zeitpolice). Under the latter all shipments are automatically held covered (gedeckt) as soon as the risk (Risiko) commences. As each shipment goes forward, a declaration of shipment (Versandbestätigung) is made by the policy holder (Versicherungsnehmer) to the underwriter (Versicherer) and the sum insured is reduced by the amount of each shipment.
The insurer issues insurance certificates (Versicherungszertifikate) covering each shipment in the case of either type of policy. The risks covered vary. The choice is usually between 'F.P.A.' and 'all risks' terms. Under an F.P.A.—free of particular average—policy (Versicherung ohne

Particular Harvarie or Frei von Beschädigung ausser im Strandungsfall) the underwriters are not liable for 'particular', i.e. partial losses (Teilschaden) except (ausser) in the case of certain risks. These include stranding (Strandung), sinking (Versenkung), burning (Verbrennen) or collision (Schiffzusammenstoss). This is the cheapest form of insurance and is suitable for bulk goods.

Under an 'all risks' policy ('all risks' Police) the underwriters pay for all loss or damage, even if partial, unless caused by delay (Verzögerung) or inherent vice or nature of the subject matter insured (innerer Verderb oder natürliche Beschaffenheit des versicherten Gegenstandes).

A less commonly used type of cover is known as W.P.A.—with particular average—(Versicherung mit Havarie or Frei von Beschädigung wenn unter 3%). This means that underwriters are liable for all losses, including 'particular' losses, i.e. partial loss or damage accidentally caused to a particular parcel of goods by perils insured against. In accordance with the German A.D.S. (Allgemeine Deutsche Seeversicherung) rules, most German insurers add a clause excluding damage under 3%.

All these types of insurance give cover against General Average (Grosse oder allgemeine Harvarie). This is damage or loss which affects the whole expedition, ship and cargo (Schiff und Ladung). It is a voluntary sacrifice made by the captain in the common interest (allgemeines Interesse) in order to avoid danger.

3. *Conditions of purchase (Einkaufsbedingungen)*

An order will usually include the following clauses:

Order (Bestellung): Only written (schriftliche) signed (mit Unterschrift versehene) orders are valid (haben Gültigkeit).

Price alterations (Preisänderungen): Price increases (Preiserhöhungen) must be expressly (ausdrücklich) agreed (anerkannt).

Price reductions (Preisermässigungen): Should the market situation (Marktlage) make a reduction (Ermässigung) of our list price (Listenpreis) necessary, the price is to be reduced accordingly.

Guarantee (Gewährleistung): The supplier guarantees (übernimmt Gewähr) his deliveries in accordance with the law (gemäss der gesetzlichen Vorschriften). He is bound (ist verpflichtet) to replace (ersetzen) on demand (auf Anforderung) free of charge (kostenlos) goods with faults (Mängel/mangelhafte Ware) which may not be immediately noticeable (erkennbar), as soon as their unserviceability (Unbrauchbarkeit) is determined (festgestellt).

Delivery (Lieferzeit): Not keeping to the agreed delivery terms (Nichteinhalten der vereinbarten Lieferfristen) entitles us to withdraw from the contract forthwith and without extension (ohne Inverzugsetzung und Nachfristsetzung von Vertrag zurückzutreten) and to claim damages for non-fulfilment (Schadenersatz wegen Nichterfüllung verlangen). 'Force Majeure' (höhere Gewalt) only relieves the supplier if he advises of the circumstances as soon as he is in a position to do so.

Place of completion (*Erfüllungsort*) and *jurisdiction* (*Gerichtsstand*): This is, unless otherwise agreed, the place to which the goods are to be delivered in accordance with the order (bestellungsgemäss), if German law (deutsches Recht) applies (ist massgebend).

Letters concerning Documents, Insurance and Terms of Sale

1. We refer to your order No. 8432 and beg to enclose the movement certificate.

   Mit Bezug auf Ihre Bestellung Nr. 8432 erlauben wir uns die Warenverkehrsbescheinigung beizulegen.

2. We refer to your order No. 8432 and request you to let us know the import-licence number as soon as possible.

   Mit Bezug auf Ihren Auftrag Nr. 8432 möchten wir Sie bitten uns die Einfuhrbewilligungsnummer sobald wie möglich bekannt zu geben.

3. We confirm with thanks receipt of your order No. 8432, but we must advise you that we are not in agreement with your terms of purchase.

   Wir bestätigen dankend den Erhalt Ihrer Bestellung Nr. 8432, möchten aber höflichst darauf hinweisen, dass wir mit den von Ihnen vorgeschlagenen Einkaufsbedingungen nicht einverstanden sind.

4. As requested, we have now arranged insurance and will attach the policy to the despatch documents.

   Wir haben Ihrem Wunsch entsprechend die Versicherung hier abgeschlossen und werden die Police den Versandpapieren beilegen.

5. We have noted that you are covering insurance yourselves.

   Wir haben zur Kenntnis genommen, dass Sie selbst für die Versicherung Sorge tragen werden.

6

Der Transport und die Verpackung

STEINEMANN: Also gut, Herr Baxter. Und wie steht es mit dem Transport? Ich nehme an, Sie wollen uns die Ware per Bahn⁽¹⁾ schicken?
BAXTER: Ja, das könnten wir eventuell machen. Wir könnten die Sendungen zum Internationalen Fracht Terminal in London liefern. Als Eilgut würde die Ware dann etwa sechs Tage später bei Ihnen sein.
STEINEMANN: Wenn alles gut geht! Aber das wäre ja wohl zu bezweifeln. Ausserdem ist das Bruchrisiko zu hoch—von Diebstahl ganz zu schweigen! Wäre Luftfracht⁽²⁾ nicht die bessere Lösung?
BAXTER: Gewiss, Herr Steinemann. Die B.A. holt sogar die Sendungen von unserer Fabrik ab. Die Ware wird über Nacht transportiert und würde am folgenden Morgen auf dem Düsseldorfer Flughafen zu Ihrer Verfügung stehen. Sehr praktisch....
STEINEMANN: ... aber wesentlich teurer, wie?
BAXTER: Ja, das kann man wohl sagen. Der Preisunterschied ist erheblich. Aber es gibt noch eine andere Möglichkeit. Wie wäre es mit dem Container-Dienst?⁽³⁾ Sehr zuverlässig und weitaus billiger!
STEINEMANN: So?
BAXTER: Ja. Jeder Container wird im Container-Umschlagplatz zollamtlich untersucht und dann plombiert. Das bürgt für zusätzliche Sicherheit gegen Diebstahl und schliesst weitere zeitraubende Zollkontrollen⁽⁴⁾ aus. Bei einem Transport mittels Bahn und Schiff könnte der Container dann zwei Tage später in Dortmund sein.
STEINEMANN: Ja, Sie meinen wohl den 'Intercontainer'-Dienst der Deutschen Bundesbahn. Der soll ja wohl sehr zuverlässig sein. Trotzdem, ich denke da noch an eine andere Transportmöglichkeit. Wie wäre es mit RoRo-Frachtern⁽⁵⁾? Ich glaube, die sind noch schneller.
BAXTER: Ja, das könnte sein. Es gibt viele solche Frachter. Wir haben gute Verbindungen mit einem Fernspediteur, der täglich LKWs mit Anhängern nach Deutschland schickt.
STEINEMANN: Sie könnten also diese Beförderungsart empfehlen?

Mr Baxter discusses with Herr Steinemann, the Head Buyer, the alternative methods of despatching the goods. They discuss the relative merits of carriage by rail, air, container and road. They also decide on the type of packaging to be used.

BAXTER: Gewiss. Man hat den grossen Vorteil, dass die Waren von Haus zu Haus geliefert werden. Ausserdem kennt man den Fahrer und kann sich auf sichere Handhabung und unverzügliche Lieferung verlassen.
STEINEMANN: Und wie lange dauert der Transport?
BAXTER: Ungefähr drei Tage.
STEINEMANN: Das scheint ja wohl dann die beste Lösung zu sein. . . .
BAXTER: Ja, das denke ich auch. Wir werden also die erste Sendung per Güterfernverkehr schicken.
STEINEMANN: Gut. Aber, Herr Baxter, vergessen Sie nicht die Heizlüfter richtig zu verpacken. Wir haben schon manche schlechte Erfahrung mit importierten Waren gemacht: Beschädigung, Korrosion, Verluste, usw. usw.
BAXTER: Herr Steinemann! Wir sind uns der Wichtigkeit zweckmässiger *Verpackung*[6] vollauf bewusst! Die Geräte werden einzeln in Kartons abgepackt und 20 solcher *Kartons* kommen dann in eine *Sperrholzkiste*. Diese Kisten sind sehr stabil und reichen für Strassengüterverkehr vollkommen aus.
STEINEMANN: Na, hoffentlich! Aber vergessen wir doch das Leitwort nicht: 'Falsch verpacken heisst Verluste erleiden, Richtig verpacken: Verluste vermeiden!'

Vocabulary

die **Abfertigung:** clearance, forwarding
der **Absender:** consignor, shipper
der **Absenderspediteur:** forwarding carrier
der **Agent:** agent
der **Anschluss:** connection
der **Auftraggeber:** consignor, principal (or agent)
die **Ausfuhr:** export
auspacken: to unpack

mit der Bahn schicken: to send by rail
der **(Bahn) Frachtbrief:** (rail) consignment note
der **Ballen:** bale
befördern: to transport, to ship
die **Beförderung:** carriage, forwarding
direkte Beförderung: direct dispatch
der **Behälter:** container
der **Behälterverkehr:** container traffic
der **Behälterumschlagplatz:** container depot *(transfer)*
behandeln: to handle
beladen: to load
die **Beschädigung:** damage
die **Bundesbahn:** German State Railway
bürgen: to vouch for, to guarantee

der **Chartervertrag:** the charter party
der **Container:** container
offener Container: open-top container
Container mit Seitentüren: container with side doors
die **Container-Abfertigungsanlage:** container (dispatch) depot (with customs office)
die **Container Anlage:** container depot
der **Containerdienst:** container service
das **Container-Depot:** container depot
der **Container-Lagerplatz:** container depot
der **Container-Sammelgutverkehr:** container groupage traffic
der **Container-Schnellzug:** container express train
das **Container-Spezialfahrzeug:** special container vehicle

das **Container-Terminal:** container terminal
der **Container-Transport:** container transport
der **Container-Umschlagplatz:** container (transfer) depot

der **Deckel:** lid, cover
die **Deutsche Bundesbahn:** German State Railway
die **Dockanlage:** dock
der **Dockarbeiter:** docker
die **Durchfahrt:** transit
die **Durchfuhr:** transit
der **Durchgangstarif:** through rate
der **Durchgangswagen:** through railway-wagon
durchgehender Container-Transport: through-container-transport
das **Düsenflugzeug:** jet plane

das **Eilgut:** express goods
der **Eilgüterzug:** fast goods train
die **Einfuhr:** import
die **Einheitsladung:** unit load
einpacken: to pack
das **Einschreibepäckchen:** registered packet
das **Einschreibepaket:** registered parcel
eintreffen (in): to arrive (at a destination)
die **Einwegkiste:** non-returnable box
die **Eisenbahnbeförderung:** railway transport
das **Eisenbahn-Container Schiff:** container rail-ferry
der **Eisenbahnfähre-Sammelwaggon:** rail-ferry container wagon
der **Empfänger:** recipient, consignee
der **Endlader:** container with doors at rear or both ends
entladen: to unload
die **Exportkiste:** export packing case
die **Exportverpackung:** export packing
das **Expressgut:** express parcel service
der **Fährboot-Waggon:** train ferry wagon
die **Fähre:** ferry (-boat)
das **Fährschiff:** ferry or train ferry

DER TRANSPORT UND DIE VERPACKUNG

das Fahrzeug: vehicle
das begleitete Fahrzeug: driver-accompanied vehicle
der Fernspediteur: long-distance haulier
die Fibertrommel: fibre-drum (for packing)
der FLEI-Verkehr (Flugzeug/Eisenbahnverkehr): air/rail traffic
die Fluglinie: airline
die Flugverkehrsgesellschaft: airline
das Flugzeug: aeroplane
die Fracht: freight
der Frachtbrief: consignment note
fracht-frei: carriage paid
der Frachtführer: freight carrier
Fracht gegen Nachnahme: freight forward
das Frachtgut: freight, cargo
die Frachtkosten: freight charges
allgemeine Frachtraten: general cargo rates
das Frachtschiff: cargo boat
der Frachtvertrag: contract of carriage

der Gabelstapler: forklift truck
der General Cargo Box Container: general cargo box container
geprüft: checked
das Gewicht: weight
der Güterfernverkehr: long-distance road haulage
der Güterzug: goods train

die Hafenanlagen: docks
die Hafengebühren: port dues
einen Hafen anlaufen: to call at a port
der Haus-Haus Transport: door-to-door transport
die Hecktür: rear door
die Holzfaserkiste: wood-fibre box
der Holzverschlag: wooden crate

der Kai: quay
der Kai-Empfangsschein: mate's receipt
der Karton: carton, cardboard box
die Kartonage: cardboard containers
die Kiste: box
die hölzerne Kiste: wooden box
der Klimaschutz: tropical protection

der Korrosionsschutz: corrosion protection
der (Kraftfahrzeug)-Anhänger: lorry trailer
das Kubikmass: cubic measure
der Kühl-Container: refrigerated container
der Kunststoff: plastic
die Kunststoff-Folie: plastic foil
der Kunststoff-Lack: synthetic varnish

die Ladeeinheit: unit load
laden: to load
der Laderaum: cargo hold
das Ladeverzeichnis: manifest
die (volle) Ladung: full load
die Lagergebühren: storage charges or costs
die Lagerung: storage
LASH-Frachter (Schuten auf Seeschiff): LASH lighter aboard ship
die Last: load
der Lastkraftwagen (LKW): lorry
der Lastzug: trailer-tractor unit
die Lattenkiste: crate
löschen: to unload a ship
der Luft-Expressdienst: air express service
die Luft-Expressfracht: express airfreight
die Luftfracht: airfreight
der Luftfrachtbrief: air waybill
die Luftfrachtgesellschaft: air-cargo carrier
das Luftfrachtkontor: airway service office
der Luftfrachtspediteur: airway forwarding agent
die Luftpaketpost: air parcel post
die Luftverkehrsgesellschaft: airline
auf dem Luftweg: by air

die Markierung: marking (on a package, etc.)
die Massengüter: bulk goods
motorisiert: motorised, tractor-drawn

(Fracht) gegen Nachnahme: freight forward

'oben': 'this side up'

das Paket: parcel
als Paket schicken: by parcel post
die Palette: pallet
der Pappkarton: cardboard box
die Pappkiste: cardboard case
die Pappschachtel: cardboard box
die Pauschalfracht: lump-sum freight
die Plombe: seal (usually of lead)
plombiert: sealed
die Post: postal service, post office
prüfen: to check
das Prüfen: checking

der Rauminhalt: capacity, volume
die Reederei: shipping company
das Rollgeld: cartage
der Ro-Ro Frachter: roll-on/roll-off ferry ship

der Sammelgutverkehr: groupage traffic
die Sammelladung: groupage consignment
der Sammeltransport: collective or groupage transport
durchgehend pallattisierter Service: through pallet service
schicken: to send
die Schiffahrtsgesellschaft: shipping company
'in Schiffswahl': a shipowner has the right to decide whether the goods are to be charged by volume or weight
der Schuppen: shed
der Schutz: protection
schützen: to protect
die Schweizer Bundesbahn (S.B.B.): Swiss State Railway
die Schwingungen: vibrations
die Seefrachtrate: seafreight rate
seefrachtmässig: seaworthy
seetüchtig: seaworthy
die Sondervorschrift: special rule or regulation
der Spediteur: carrier or forwarding agent
die internationale Spedition: international forwarding

der Speditionsvertrag: contract of carriage
das Sperrgut: bulky goods
die Sperrholzkiste: plywood case
die Stahlbandverschnürung: steel bands (for securing a case)
der Standard Stahl-Container: standard steel container
der Stoss (pl. Stösse): knock, impact(s)
die Stossfestigkeit: impact resistance
der Strassengüterverkehr: road haulage
das Stückgut: piece goods

die Tara (Gewicht): tare (weight)
das Teerpapier: tarred paper
die Tragfähigkeit: carrying capacity
der Trailer: trailer
der Traktor: tractor
die Transportkosten: transport costs, cartage
das Transportunternehmen: haulage firm
der Transportunternehmer: haulier

die Überseezeit: ferry time
übertragen: to transfer
umladen: to transfer, to reload

der Verderb: destruction
verladen: to load
die Verladung: loading
der Verlust: loss
die Vernagelung: nailing
verpacken: to pack
die Verpackung: packing
die innere Verpackung: inner packing
Verpackung besonders berechnet: packing charged extra
Verpackung zum Wegwerfen: non-returnable packing
die Versandanweisungen: forwarding instructions
die Versandanzeige: dispatch note
die Versandspesen: forwarding charges
die Versandvorschriften: forwarding instructions
die Verschiffung: shipment, shipping
die Verwaltungskosten: handling charges
VORSICHT! (auf Kisten): TAKE CARE! (on boxes)

wasserdicht: watertight, waterproof
die Wellpappe: corrugated paper

zerbrechlich: fragile
zerlegen: to dismantle/knock down (a piece of machinery)
Zoll einrichten: to clear customs
die Zollabfertigung: customs clearance
der Zollagent: customs agent
das Zollamt: customs office
der Zollmakler: customs house broker
das Zollsiegel: customs seal

der Zollverschluss: customs seal
der Zug: train
der durchgehende Zug: through-train
zusammenfassen: to group or combine
zusammenstellen: to group or combine (various loads)
einwandfreier Zustand: perfect condition
die Zustellung: delivery
zuverlässig: safe, reliable
die Zwischenlandung: intermediate landing, stop-over

Commercial Notes on Transport

In deciding the most suitable method of transport, the following are usually the main considerations:

(a) Speed (Geschwindigkeit)

(b) Security (Sicherheit)

(c) Cost (Kosten)

The value and nature of the goods (Wert und Art der Ware) and the buyer's instructions (Anweisungen) may also be factors. The following are the four main methods of transport to the Continent:

1. *Rail Transport (Bahntransport)*
    Goods can be consigned (ausgeliefert) to distributors in Germany direct by rail service through British Rail. Consignments (Sendungen) travel by train-ferry wagon (Fährboot-Waggon). Groupage facilities (Sammelgutverkehr) for loads (Ladungen) of less than a full wagon load (Waggonladung) are organised by forwarding agents (Spediteure) in conjunction with British Rail. The London International Freight Terminal—LIFT—(Internationales Fracht-Terminal) at Stratford, London, was established by British Rail to deal with both full (Voll-) and part (Teil-) wagon loads (Waggonladungen) of goods travelling to and from Europe and to deal also with freight-container loads (Fracht-Container Ladungen) and TIR road vehicles (Fahrzeuge) and trailers (Anhänger). Customs clearance (Zollabfertigung) is dealt with by British Rail.
    There are three principal methods of forwarding goods by rail. Ordinary goods (Frachtgut), fast goods (Eilgut), and international express parcels carried by passenger train (Expressgut). Such traffic is consigned throughout the journey under the 'Conditions of the International Convention concerning the Carriage of Goods by Rail'

(C.I.M.). Only one International consignment note (Frachtbrief) is required and conveyance under this convention (Abkommen) is at British Rail's risk (auf das Risiko von British Rail). Goods may also be consigned from principal industrial centres (Haupt-Industriezentren) in the U.K. to almost any destination in Germany. Typical transit times (Transit-Zeiten) quoted for goods sent as 'Frachtgut' are 7 days to Hamburg and 6 days to Frankfurt. In the case of rail-express parcels (Expressgut), British Rail quotes a figure of 24 hours for every 400 km of the journey plus 48 hours for the sea crossing (Seeüberfahrt).

2. *Airfreight* (*Luftfracht*)

In spite of its higher cost (höhere Kosten) this method may be preferable if time is important. It is particularly suitable for consignments (Sendungen) of low weight (geringes Gewicht) and high value (hoher Wert). Packing costs (Verpackungskosten) are lower and the security (Sicherheit) of the goods is greater.

There are three alternative services:

(a) Scheduled air cargo services (planmässige Luftverkehrsdienste) operated by B.A., Lufthansa and other airlines (Fluggesellschaften).

(b) Air charter (Charterflugzeug); the exporter charters (chartert) a whole aircraft (ein ganzes Flugzeug) or shares (teilt) the hire with other exporters.

(c) Airtaxi (Flugtaxe)—for small consignments (kleine Sendungen) from minor airfields (Flugfelder).

The exporter can either deliver (senden) the goods to the airport (Flughafen) or have them collected (abholen lassen), by B.A. (in London or within five miles of their airports) or by B.R.S. or one of the specialist air-freight carriers (Luftfracht-Transportgesellschaften). Prepaid consignments (vorausbezahlte Sendungen) can also be dispatched (abgeschickt) to B.A. from all rail parcel stations (Bahnhof Paketannahme). On delivery to B.A. goods must be accompanied by a fully completed air waybill (Luftfrachtbrief) or an instruction for dispatch (Versandanweisungs-formular) from which the airline will complete the air waybill (Luftfrachtbrief). B.A. operate a 'through pallet service' (durchgehend palletisierter Service) from London, Manchester, Birmingham and Glasgow to most large European cities. Loads (Ladungen) are assembled (zusammengestellt) at these airports and transferred (übertragen) to the scheduled (planmässig) overnight cargo flights (Frachtflüge). Freight carried on these services is available at the consignee's (Empfängers) nearest airport during the early hours of the following morning. It can either be collected by the consignee, if he requires the goods urgently, or delivered during the day of arrival. Thus a one-day service is normally effected.

3. *Container* (*Behälter/Container*)

Containers offer many advantages, particularly if the exporter can provide a full load (volle Ladung). If he has only a part-load (Teilladung), this is grouped (gesammelt) with consignments (Sendungen) from other exporters at inland container depots (Inland-Container-Umschlagplätze) by container operators (Container-Spediteure). The containers are customs-inspected (zollamtlich untersucht/geprüft) and sealed (plombiert) at the terminal (Terminal) before they start on their journey to the port, thus avoiding the need for further examination (Untersuchung).

One of the main advantages of sending goods by container is the security (Sicherheit) resulting from a sealed unit (plombierte Einheit) which cannot be opened without detection, and the reduced handling (Handhabung) of individual items. This enables packing (Verpackung) to be reduced and effects cost savings (Kosteneinsparungen) in packing materials (Verpackungsmaterialien) and in freight costs (Frachtkosten), due to reduced weight (geringeres Gewicht). Furthermore, because units can be customs sealed (plombiert) and can travel under TIR conditions, additional customs examinations at en-route frontier crossings (Grenzüberschreitungen) are virtually eliminated (ausgeschlossen). All this makes for a very much increased speed of transit (schnellerer Verkehr). Containers normally conform to I.S.O. (International Standard) dimensions (Abmessungen) and specifications (technische Daten). I.S.O. Standard external dimensions (Aussenmasse) are 8 ft in width (Breite), 8 ft or 8 ft 6 inches in height (Höhe) and 20 ft, 30 ft or 40 ft in length (Länge).

The most common type of container is a simple box construction with a door at one end (Hecktür). Other types have doors at both ends (End-Lader) and/or side doors (Seitentüren). Then there are containers with open tops (oben offen) and others which are insulated (isoliert) or refrigerated (gekühlt).

Containers are carried inland (im Binnenland) by either rail or road transport (Eisenbahn- oder Strassenverkehr) to the ports where they are either loaded directly on to the container ship (sofort auf das Containerschiff verladen) or they travel throughout on the road vehicle or its trailer (auf dem Lastwagen oder dessen Anhänger) via the Cross-Channel roll-on, roll-off ferry ships (Ro-Ro Frachter).

Within Europe the 'Intercontainer' network, operated by 19 national railway systems, provides express train services (Expressgutverkehr) between major industrial centres. Intercontainer quotes 'through tariffs' (Durchgangstarife) and issues single consignment notes (Frachtbriefe) for each container.

Transit times (Transitzeiten) for containerised consignments to Germany vary according to the destination (Bestimmungsort), the inland transport mode (Binnentransportart) used to get the container to and from the port and the channel crossing route (Kanalüberfahrt Route) selected.

4. *Road Transport (Strassengüterverkehr)*

Goods can be sent either on driver-accompanied vehicles (begleitete Fahrzeuge) through to their destination or on unaccompanied trailers (unbegleitete Anhänger), which are delivered by European transport operators (Speditionsgesellschaften). There are a large number of cross-channel roll-on, roll-off ferry services (Ro-Ro Fähren) offering a rapid door-to-door (Haus zu Haus) service. This method of transport can have a number of important advantages:

(i) Goods are not off-loaded (entladen) or re-handled (umgeladen) during transit.

(ii) Expensive packing (teure Verpackung) is not required.

(iii) The exporter is in direct contact with (steht in direkter Verbindung mit) the person responsible (verantwortlich) for the load (Ladung) and can be reasonably confident about its safe treatment (zuverlässige Handhabung) and prompt delivery (sofortige Lieferung).

(iv) The system is flexible (abänderungsfähig) and the load does not have to wait to be fitted in with scheduled services (planmässige Transporte).

(v) When the exporter has only a part-load (Teilladung) the haulier (Spediteur) will seek more traffic to make a full load (volle Ladung) so that the exporter does not have to bear the total hire cost (Mietpreis) of the vehicle.

(vi) The transport operator will select the most suitable and economic combination of inland route (Binnenroute), cross-channel service (Kanalüberfahrt) and overland route (Überlandweg) in Europe and he will quote a through rate (Durchgangstarif).

In the case of goods carried by unaccompanied trailer many of these advantages still apply. However, the responsibility (Verantwortung) for the delivery (Zustellung) of the goods will be shared (geteilt) between the U.K. haulier and the European haulier (Spediteur) and this may result in delays.

Transit times for driver-accompanied vehicles vary, but generally a load would be delivered in Cologne or Frankfurt on the second day after collection. All vehicles operate under the T.I.R. (Transport International Routier) system, whereby a carnet avoids customs examination at intermediate frontiers.

5. *Seafreight* (*Seefracht*)

Freighting of general cargo (gemischte Ladungen) to Europe by conventional seafreight is no longer an economic proposition. Apart from bulk commodities (Massengüter) almost all goods are dispatched by container or in roll-on/roll-off vehicles (RoRo-Fahrzeuge). The advent of container ships (Container-Schiffe) and roll-on/roll-off ferry ships (RoRo-Frachter) with their associated dockside facilities (Kaianlagen) geared to very rapid loading (Ladearbeit) and unloading (Löscharbeit) has reduced the transit time of seaborne freight dramatically.

6. *Packing* (*Verpackung*)

External packing for export (äussere Exportverpackung) usually consists of wooden cases (Holzkisten), plywood cases (Sperrholzkisten), wooden crates (Holzverschläge), cardboard cases (Pappkisten) or cartons (Kartons), bales (Ballen), casks (Fässer), drums (Trommeln) and cans (Kanister).

Internal packing may consist of corrugated paper (Wellpappe) or of other materials such as shredded paper (Papierwolle), wood wool (Holzwolle), gummed fibres (gummierte Faser), rubber or plastic foam (Gummi- oder Kunststoffschaum) or moulded foam (fester Schaumstoff).

It may be necessary to provide protection against corrosion (Korrosionsschutz) and this may be achieved by lining (ausschlagen) the case with sheet zinc (Zinkblech) or layers of insulating material (Sperrschichtmaterial). Oily, soft or hard coatings (ölige, weiche oder harte Überzüge) can also be applied, either cold or hot, to the surface which has to be protected.

Other protective materials include plastic varnishes (Kunststofflacke), strip coatings (Abziehlacke), wax dips (Tauchwachs), plastic foils (Kunststoff-Folien), silica gel (Kieselgel) and vapour-phase inhibitor paper (VPI-Papier).

Efficient export packing (zweckmässige Exportverpackung) will protect (schützen) goods against damage (Beschädigung) and deterioration (Verderb) and avoid loss (Verlust). In particular it should guard against impact (Stoss), vibration (Schwingung) and moisture (Feuchtigkeit).

Letters regarding Transport and Packing

1. We have dispatched to you today the following goods by express rail service; they are due to arrive on the 10th of April.

   Wir haben heute an Ihre Adresse die folgende Sendung per Eilgut versandt. Ankunft ist für den 10. April vorgesehen.

2. The difference in freight rates between goods train and passenger train is very considerable. We have investigated the cost of road transport and would suggest this to be the better alternative.

   Der Preisunterschied zwischen Gütertransport und Eilgut ist sehr erheblich. Wir haben die Kosten für Lastwagentransport ermittelt und möchten vorschlagen, die Ware auf diesem Wege zu senden.

3. We are supplying the fan heaters in cartons.

   Wir liefern die Heizlüfter in Kartons.

4. If not returned to us by the 30th of June the cases will be charged to you at DM 5.— each.

   Falls die Kisten nicht bis zum 30. Juni an uns zurückgesandt werden, werden sie mit je DM 5.— berechnet.

5. Please debit us with cartage between the airport and the depot.

   Wir möchten Sie bitten uns mit den Transportkosten vom Flugplatz zum Depot zu belasten.

7

Der Handelsvertretungsvertrag

BAXTER: Wir sind uns also einig, Herr Withof, dass Sie unsere Vertretung übernehmen?
WITHOF: Im Prinzip, ja, Herr Baxter. Nur müssen wir uns zuerst über einige Grundgedanken klar sein.
BAXTER: Natürlich. Was möchten Sie zuerst besprechen?
WITHOF: Herr Baxter, nach den Kundenbesuchen die wir gemacht haben werden Sie sich sicher des entscheidenden Merkmals[1] des deutschen Markts bewusst geworden sein. Ich meine den harten Wettbewerb!
BAXTER: Ja, das kann man wohl sagen.
WITHOF: Dies bedeutet, dass die Stellung des Käufers sehr stark ist. Mit anderen Worten: der Kunde ist bei uns König. Er hat eine grosse Auswahl unter zahlreichen deutschen und ausländischen Firmen und um konkurrieren zu können müssen wir eine Vertrauensbasis bei den Kunden schaffen. Und das verlangt Zeit—und Geduld! Zuerst kommen nur kleine Aufträge und es dauert mehrere Jahre, ehe wir mit einem beträchtlichen Umsatz rechnen können.
BAXTER: Ja, das ist mir klar. Aber wie lange soll diese Einführungszeit dauern?
WITHOF: Das ist schwer zu sagen, Herr Baxter. Ich denke, dass wir mit mindestens zweieinhalb Jahren rechnen müssen.
BAXTER: Zweieinhalb Jahre! Könnte es wirklich nicht etwas schneller sein?
WITHOF: Vielleicht, Herr Baxter, wenn wir Glück haben. Aber vieles hängt natürlich von Ihrer Leistung ab. Wenn Sie schnell Muster liefern; wenn Sie die vereinbarten Liefertermine einhalten; wenn Sie Anfragen und Reklamationen unverzüglich erledigen—dann könnte es eventuell schneller gehen!
BAXTER: Wir werden unser Möglichstes tun.
WITHOF: Gut. Könnten wir jetzt einmal kurz den Handelsvertretungsvertrag[2] besprechen? Sie erwähnten, dass Sie einen Vertragsentwurf mitgebracht hätten?

Mr Baxter is now back in Herr Withof's office at Scheerer Elektro-Geräte. They agree that Scheerer Elektro-Geräte will represent Mayheat in certain areas of Germany and Herr Withof explains some of the difficulties of introducing a new product in the German market. They discuss some of the clauses which will be included in the agency contract.

BAXTER: Stimmt. Hier ist er. Sehen wir mal hier: der Bezirk.$^{(2.5)}$ Der soll wohl Nordrhein-Westfalen, Niedersachsen und Schleswig-Holstein sein, nicht wahr?

WITHOF: Wir könnten Rheinland-Pfalz einschliessen und auch Hessen, wenn Sie wollen.

BAXTER: Nicht gleich zuviel auf einmal, Herr Withof! Ich glaube, drei Länder sind vorerst einmal genug. Und wie steht es mit der Provision?$^{(2.8)}$ Ich meine, für die Ware die wir direkt an die Kunden liefern.

WITHOF: Wie gesagt, die beträgt 25%.

BAXTER: Vorläufig gesagt, Herr Withof! Und das war der Aufschlag auf den Einstandspreis. Sie entspricht also 20% des Verkaufspreises.

WITHOF: Ja, wenn Sie es so ausdrücken. Also: 20% Ihres fakturierten Preises zum Kunden.

BAXTER: Halbjährlich$^{(2.8d)}$ zahlbar! Einverstanden?

WITHOF: Wir sind an vierteljährliche Abrechnung gewöhnt, Herr Baxter.

BAXTER: Sie sind ein harter Mann, Herr Withof! Na ja . . . sagen wir vierteljährlich. Und die Dauer des Vertrages$^{(2.12)}$. . . . Ich möchte vorschlagen, dass wir eine Probezeit von einem Jahr haben. Danach könnten wir dann vielleicht von einem Vertrag auf unbestimmte Dauer sprechen.

WITHOF: Und die Kündigungsfrist?$^{(2.12)}$

BAXTER: Vorläufig 3 Monate. Ist Ihnen das recht?

WITHOF: Ja, das ist in Ordnung.

Vocabulary

der Ablauf (eines Vertrages): expiry of (a contract)
das Absatzgebiet: sales or marketing territory
abschliessen (einen Vertrag): to enter into an agreement
der Agent: agent
die Agentur: agency
der Agenturvertrag: agency agreement
die Aktiengesellschaft (A.G.): limited company
das Alleinrecht: exclusive right
das Alleinverkaufsrecht: exclusive selling right
der Alleinvertreter: exclusive agent
die Alleinvertretung: exclusive agency
aufheben (einen Vertrag): to cancel a contract
aufsetzen (einen Vertrag): to draw up (a contract)
der Auftraggeber: principal (in legal sense)
der Auftragnehmer: agent (in legal sense)
ausdrücklich: expressly
die Ausführung: design, construction, execution
der Auslandsvertreter: overseas agent

der Bankrott: bankruptcy (ordinary)
der fahrlässige Bankrott: bankruptcy (reckless)
Bankrott machen: to go or to become bankrupt
beenden (ein Vertragsverhältnis): to terminate (a contract)
bestimmen: to define
der Betriebsführer: managing director or works manager
der Betriebsleiter: works manager
der Bezirksvertreter: area agent
sich binden: to bind oneself (by contract)
die Bonität: solvency, good standing
brechen (einen Vertrag): to break a contract

die Delkredereprovision: 'del credere' commission
der Dienstvertrag: service agreement
der Dritte: third party

der Eigenhändler: businessman (trading on his own account)
das Eigentumsrecht: (right of) ownership
einhalten (eine Vertragsbestimmung): to conform or keep to a clause in a contract
die Einleitung: introduction
die Einschränkung: restriction or reservation
der Einzelhändler: retailer
entlassen: to dismiss
ernennen: to appoint
erneuern: to renew (a contract)
die Erneuerung: renewal
eröffnen (ein Geschäft): to open a shop/business
Europäische Wirtschaftsgemeinschaft (E.W.G.): European Economic Community (E.E.C.)

der Fachkaufmann: specialist
die Fahrlässigkeit: negligence
grobe Fahrlässigkeit: gross negligence
fällig: due
(als) Fideikommiss besitzen: to hold in trust
die Filiale: branch (legally dependent on parent company)
finanziell: financial
imaterieller Firmenwert: goodwill of a business
fristlos: without notice

die Garantie: guarantee
garantieren: to guarantee
der Garantievertreter: 'del credere' agent
das Gebrauchsmuster: sample, registered design
die Gegenleistung: return service
als Gegenleistung: in return for
das Gehalt: salary, wage
festes Gehalt: fixed salary
der Generalvertreter: general agent or sole representative
das Gericht: the court

gerichtlich gegen jemanden vorgehen: to take someone to court
der Gerichtsstand: jurisdiction
der Geschäftsführer: managing director
das Geschäftsgeheimnis: business or trade secret
die (Geschäfts) Vertragsfähigkeit: capacity to contract
die Gesetzgebung: legislation
gesetzlich: legal
gesetzlich geschützt: protected by law, patented
Gesellschaft mit beschränkter Haftung (G.m.b.H./GMBH.): limited company
höhere Gewalt: 'force majeure'

handeln: to trade
der Handelsmakler: broker
das Handelsrecht: commercial law
die Handelsspanne: (gross) margin
der Handelsvertreter: commercial agent, manufacturer's agent

der Importeur: importer
importieren: to import
die Inkassovollmacht: authority to collect (bills of exchange, etc.)

der Kommissionär: commission agent
die Konkurrenz: competition
konkurrieren: to compete
Konkurs machen: to go into bankruptcy, to go bankrupt
das Konkursverfahren (normale): (ordinary) bankruptcy
das Konsignationslager: consignment stock
in Konsignation nehmen (Waren): to take (goods) on consignment, to consign
konsignieren: to consign (goods)
die Kreditfähigkeit: credit worthiness
der Kundendienst: after-sales service
die Kündigung: dismissal
die Kündigungsfrist: period of notice
die Kundschaft: customers
die Kundschaft übernehmen: to acquire the goodwill of a business

die Lage: situation, position, standing, status

die finanzielle Lage: financial standing
von einer Liste streichen: to take off a list

massgebend: authoritative
das Mindesteinkommen: minimum income

der Nachteil: disadvantage
nachteilig: detrimental, prejudicial

offenlegen: to disclose

das Patentrecht: patent right
ein Patent verletzen: to infringe a patent
die Patentverletzung: infringement of a patent
der Platzvertreter: local agent
die Probe: sample
die Probezeit: trial period
die Provision: commission
der Provisionsvertreter: commission agent
der Provisionssatz: rate of commission

das Recht: law, right
auf eigene Rechnung handeln: to conduct business on one's own account
das massgebende Recht: applicable law
das Reisegeld: traveling allowance
die Reisespesen: travelling expenses
das Risiko: risk

der Schaden: damage
der Schadenersatz: compensation, damages
Schadenersatzklage erheben: to sue for damages
das Schiedsgericht: court of arbitration
das Schiedsverfahren: arbitration
der Sitz (einer Vertretung): head office (of an agency)
der Stammkunde: longstanding customer
streichen (von einer Liste): to withdraw (from a list)
die Streitsache: case under dispute

die Tochtergesellschaft: subsidiary company (legally independent)

treuhänderisch verwalten: to hold in trust

übernehmen (eine Vertretung): to take on (an agency)

der Umsatz: turnover

unbestimmt: indefinite

der Unternehmer: principal

der Untervertreter: sub-agent

die (Verkaufs) filiale: branch (legally dependent on parent company)

sich verpflichten: to bind oneself

der Verteiler: distributor

der Vertrag: contract

einen Vertrag aufsetzen: to draw up a contract

einen Vertrag erneuern: to renew a contract

der stillschweigend geschlossene Vertrag: tacit agreement, implied contract

Vertragsbestimmungen einhalten: to conform to the conditions of a contract

der Vertragsentwurf: draft contract

der Vertragsteilnehmer: partner (in a contract)

die Vertragsverletzung: infringement of a contract

der Vertrauensschaden: loss incurred from breach of contract

der Vertreter: representative, agent

die Vertreterbefugnisse: duties of an agent

der Vertreterbezirk: area of an agency

die Vertreterprovision: agent's commission

die Vertretung: agency

verwalten: to administer

der Vorbehalt: reservation or restriction

vorgehen (gegen jemanden gerichtlich): to institute (legal proceedings against someone)

das Vorkommnis: event

die Vorschrift: rule, decree

das geschäftsführende Vorstandsmitglied: managing director

die Währung: currency

das Warenausgangskonto: account sales

der Warenbestand: stock, inventory

der Warenempfänger: consignee

das Warenzeichen: trade-mark

das Warenzeichen, eingetragene: registered trade-mark

der Wettbewerb: competition

der Wettbewerb, unlautere: unfair competition

auf unbestimmte Zeit: for an indefinite period

die Zweigniederlassung: subsidiary, branch (general terms)

Commercial Notes on Representation and Agency Contracts

1. *General*

A firm wishing to sell in West Germany can do so either through a Commercial Agent (einen Handelsvertreter), a branch (eine Zweigniederlassung), a subsidiary company (eine Tochtergesellschaft oder Filiale) or by selling directly (Direktverkauf) to wholesalers (Grosshändler), retailers (Einzelhändler) or final customers (Endverbraucher).

Most German firms—67% according to a recent survey—sell through commercial agents and this is usually the best way for a foreign firm (ausländische Firma) to approach the market.

The decisive characteristic of the German market is very severe competition (Wettbewerb/Konkurrenz). As a result the buyer (Käufer) is in a strong position, for he nearly always has a choice (Auswahl) between different German and foreign suppliers (Lieferfirmen), all striving to obtain his orders (die sich alle um seine Aufträge bemühen). On the other hand he must choose carefully (sorgfältig wählen), because he likewise has to compete with his goods (mit seinen Waren im Wettbewerb bestehen).

The first task of the agent is to create a basis of trust (eine Vertrauensbasis schaffen) between the firms he represents (die Firmen die er vertritt) and his customers (seine Kunden). In most cases the first orders (ersten Aufträge) are only submitted, because the customer relies on the advice of the agent (verlässt sich auf den Rat des Handelsvertreters). Therefore the agent must know what he is offering (was er anbietet) and what the foreign firm which he is representing can do (leisten kann). In the first place a thorough discussion (eine gründliche Aussprache) with the representative is absolutely necessary, so that the production programme (das Produktionsprogramm) as well as the conditions of delivery (Lieferbedingungen) and the terms of payment (Zahlungsbedingungen) can be discussed (erörtert werden), the methods of transport (Transportarten) explained and advice given about the presentation (Aufmachung) and publicity (Werbung) for the product. The agent will also need to know something about the technical characteristics of the goods (die technische Zusammensetzung der Ware) and their practical application (ihre Verwendungsmöglichkeiten), so that he can advise (beraten) his customers. The significance of the function of German agents can be judged from the fact that they are responsible for an annual turnover of goods (einen jährlichen Warenumsatz) amounting to DM 140,000 m (140 Milliarden).

At first, however, only small orders (kleine Aufträge) can be expected and a preliminary period (Einführungszeit) of from one to two years is always necessary for establishing business connections (Geschäftsverbindungen aufzubauen). If good results are to be expected the principal must supply samples (Muster) on time (rechtzeitig). Subsequent deliveries must be in accordance with the samples (mustergetreu) and the delivery dates agreed (die vereinbarten Liefertermine) adhered to (eingehalten werden). Enquiries (Anfragen) and complaints (Reklamationen) must be dealt with without delay (unverzüglich erledigt werden). From the legal (rechtlich) and economic (wirtschaftlich) point of view the German commercial agent is an independent businessman (ein selbständiger Geschäftsmann), who takes over the task (übernimmt die Aufgabe) of furthering and promoting the sales of those firms he represents in his area (den Absatz der von ihm vertretenen Firmen in seinem Bezirk) and advising the firms and the customers as a specialist (sachgemäss zu beraten). This means that the firms represented have to pay no taxes (Steuern) or insurance contributions (Sozialversicherungsbeiträge) on behalf of the agents. It is customary for the agent to represent several manufacturing firms (mehrere Industriefirmen) so that the products he offers are complementary to each other (sich gegenseitig ergänzen).

The area (Bezirk) which the agent is to cover (bearbeiten soll) must be agreed on during the preliminary negotiations (Verhandlungen). Sometimes a firm will be in contact (in Verbindung stehen) with only one agent in the Federal Republic (Bundesrepublik) and he in turn works with other colleagues (mit anderen Kollegen). In many cases, however, different representatives are appointed (beauftragt) for the most important areas (die wichtigsten Bezirke). Agreements (Vereinbarungen) with agents are usually in the form of written contracts (schriftliche Verträge). An example of such a contract in German, with an English translation, is given at the end of this chapter.

Remuneration (Vergütung) consists basically (grundsätzlich) of commission (Provision) and includes all business (alle Geschäfte) done within the area covered by the representative, irrespective or not whether the agent played a part in securing the business (gleichgültig, ob der Handelsvertreter daran mitwirkt oder nicht). In addition reimbursement of particular expenses (Rückerstattung bestimmter Auslagen) is usually made, for example postage (Porto) and telephone expenses (Fernsprechkosten) and also remuneration for noteworthy achievements (besondere Leistungen), if that should be deemed necessary in individual cases (wenn es im Einzelfall erforderlich sein sollte). During the introductory period remuneration as a rule takes the form of a fixed allowance (fester Zuschuss) or a higher commission (zusätzliche Provision).

In individual cases it may be advisable for the manufacturer to set up a supply depot (Auslieferungslager) in Germany so that the customer can be supplied quickly (um den Kunden schnell beliefern zu können).

The above notes are condensed from a section of a booklet entitled 'Praktische Hinweise für die Vertretung ausländischer Firmen', published by the C.D.H. (Centralvereinigung Deutscher Handelsvertreter und Handelsmaklerverbände), 5, Köln 41 (Lindenthal), Geleniusstrasse 1. It contains a great deal of further practical information for both agents and foreign principals. The C.D.H. publishes a journal called 'Der Handelsvertreter und Handelsmakler' and this contains a list of 'Freie Vertretungen'. Firms seeking an agent in Germany can have their names included in this list by writing to the C.D.H.

More useful information is contained in a leaflet published by the British Embassy in Bonn, entitled 'Seeking and working with a Commercial Agent in the Federal Republic of Germany'.

2. *The Agency Agreement* (*Der Handelsvertretungsvertrag*)

The agreement should be drawn up (aufgesetzt sein) with care and should contain whichever of the following clauses (Klauseln) are appropriate:

2.1 *Nature of the contract* (*Art des Vertrages*)
Whether it relates to an exclusive agency (Alleinvertretung), local agency (Bezirksvertretung) or sub-agency (Untervertretung).

2.2 *Parties to the agreement* (*Vertragspartner*)
Their names (Namen), addresses (Adressen) and capacity (Geschäftsvertragsfähigkeit) of each contracting party.

2.3 *Authentic text* (*Massgebender Text*)
If the contract is drawn up in two languages (in zwei Sprachen/zweisprachig), which of the two is authentic (massgebend) in case of dispute.

2.4 *Products covered by the contract* (*Unter den Vertrag fallende Erzeugnisse*)
The general nature (Art und Beschaffenheit) of the products covered by the contract should be stated, possibly by reference to the manufacturer's lists (Warenkataloge des Herstellers). The manufacturer's right (Recht) to withdraw products from the list (Erzeugnisse von der Liste zu streichen) should be stated (sollte festgelegt sein).

2.5 *The sales territory* (*Vertretungsgebiet oder Bezirk*) *and E.E.C. Anti-trust Legislation* (*Kartellgesetzgebung der E.W.G.*)
The territory (Bezirk) in which the agent is to act should be clearly defined (bestimmt). Consideration should be given to the possible infringement (Verletzung) of E.E.C. anti-trust laws (Antitrustgesetze). The E.E.C. regulations governing competition (Konkurrenz) include the requirement for notification to the European Communities Commission in Brussels of certain exclusive representation agreements (Alleinvertretungsverträge). As a general rule, the notification requirement does not apply to agreements with commercial agents who do not assume financial responsibility in carrying out the contract or selling the goods (auf eigene Rechnung verkaufen).

An agreement with a distributor who owns and stocks considerable quantities of goods may fall within the scope of these laws. However, exclusive distributorship agreements which conform with the E.E.C. Commission's regulation of 14th March 1967 need not be notified to the Commission. The latter regulation provides for a group of exceptions covering a very large number of agreements which involve granting by a manufacturer of exclusive rights for resale of products in a specific area of the E.E.C.

2.6　*The duties of the principal* (*Die Pflichten des Unternehmers*)

(a)　One must establish whether the principal is bound (verpflichtet) by the agent's acceptance of orders, or whether the agent must only take orders subject to his principal's acceptance (Zustimmung). In the latter case can the principal refuse to accept (die Annahme verweigern) the order without giving a reason (ohne einen Grund anzugeben)? 'Force Majeure' (höhere Gewalt) normally frees the principal from responsibility for late or non-delivery.

(b)　This covers the rights of the principal to set up a subsidiary in the territory (die Rechte des Unternehmers eine Tochtergesellschaft im Bezirk zu errichten) or to make sales to the territory other than through the agent. It should also lay down whether all enquiries received direct by the principal are to be referred (verwiesen) to the agent.

(c)　*Information* (*Information*)
The duty of the principal to advise (benachrichtigen) in good time (rechtzeitig) of all changes in the product or in the price, delivery or terms of sale.

(d)　*Provision of samples, publicity material, etc.* (*Versorgung mit Proben, Mustern, Drucksachen, Werbematerial usw.*)

(e)　*Allowance for overheads and expenses* (*Vergütung von Unkosten und Auslagen*)
To what extent the principal agrees to re-imburse (vergüten) travelling expenses (Reisekosten), telephone calls (Telefongebühren), telegrams (Telegramme), etc.

(f)　*Unfair competition* (*unlauterer Wettbewerb*)
The obligation of the principal to prevent unfair competition in the market, such as the infringement of patents (Patentverletzung), or the use of trade marks (eingetragene Warenzeichen), signs (Kennzeichen), designs (Gebrauchsmuster) or other exclusive rights (Alleinrechte).

(g)　*Exceptions, reserves or restrictions* (*Ausnahmen, Vorbehalte, Einschränkungen*)
Long-standing customers (Stammkunden), other agreements (andere Verträge), etc.

2.7 The duties of the agent (die Pflichten des Vertreters)

(a) *The power of the agent to engage the principal* (das Abschlussrecht des Vertreters)
The agent not to pledge the principal's credit (auf Kredit des Auftraggebers einkaufen) or to commence legal proceedings (gerichtlich vorgehen) without the principal's consent (ohne die Genehmigung des Auftraggebers).

(b) *Prohibition of competition* (Konkurrenzverbot)
Is the agent permitted to take on other agencies which might compete (konkurrieren) with the one in the contract? If not, the period during which the prohibition extends; this may be beyond the expiry of the agreement. If the principal cannot meet competition (gegen eine Konkurrenz aufkommen) in any particular case, or for any reason be unable temporarily to supply goods, whether the agent may purchase elsewhere.

(c) *Rights or duty to use name of principal* (Recht oder Pflicht den Namen der vertretenen Firma zu verwenden)
Does the agent have the right or duty to use the principal's name on his letter-heading (Schreibkopf) and/or office name plate (Namensschild)? Is he obliged to inform third parties (Dritte) of the nature and extent (Umfang) of his powers as an agent?

(d) *Observance of terms of sale, etc.* (Einhaltung von Verkaufsbedingungen)
The agent should conform to the principal's instructions (den Weisungen der vertretenen Firma entsprechen) with regard to prices, terms of delivery and of payment (Liefer- und Zahlungsbedingungen), warranties (Garantien), etc.

(e) *Consignment Stock* (Konsignationslager/Auslieferungslager)
A useful way of ensuring immediate delivery (sofortige Lieferung) in the market, without the agent having to tie up capital (Kapital festlegen) in stocks, is for the principal to send the agent goods on consignment (in Konsignation). Under this arrangement the goods belong to the principal (die Waren gehören dem Unternehmer). The latter can take them back if he thinks fit and the consignee (Warenempfänger) has the right to return unsold goods. The cost of transport, insurance, etc. is normally for the account of the principal (die Kosten gehen auf Rechnung der vertretenen Firma), but this must be specified in the contract. It should also be stated that the agent is not to sell consignment stocks other than as agent for the principal, that the agent should send regular inventories (Inventare) and account sales (Verkaufsabrechnungen), and that the principal has the right to check (kontrollieren) the stock at any time.

(f) *Minimum stock and turnover* (*Mindestwarenbestand und Umsatz*)
The contract may oblige the agent to keep a certain minimum stock (Mindestwarenbestand) and/or to guarantee a certain minimum turnover (Mindestumsatz). A higher rate of commission (Provisionssatz) on sales above the minimum may be arranged in return (als Gegenleistung).

(g) *After-sales Service and spare parts* (*Kundendienst und Ersatzteile*)
Does the agent agree to keep a stock of spare parts (Ersatzteillager) or to ensure a special after-sales service (Kundendienst)? If so, the extent of his obligations (den Umfang seiner Verpflichtungen), whether the spare parts are to be on consignment (konsigniert), and the remuneration (Vergütung) if any, paid by the principal to the agent for these services.

(h) *Periodical Reports* (*regelmässige Berichte*)
Whether the agent is to submit periodical reports giving information (Nachrichten) on his activities (Tätigkeit) on any changes which have taken place in the market (Marktänderungen) or in the financial standing (Kreditwürdigkeit) of his customers.

(j) *Guaranteed minimum income* (*garantiertes Mindesteinkommen*)
The principal may guarantee the agent a certain minimum income on account of commission (als Anzahlung auf seine Provision).

(k) *Trade secrets* (*Geschäftsgeheimnisse*)
The agent is forbidden to disclose (bekanntmachen) the principal's trade secrets.

2.8 *Commission* (*Provision*)
The contract should clearly state:

(a) The rate of commission (Provisionssatz).

(b) The figure (Ziffer) on which the commission is to be paid.

(c) When the commission is earned (verdient), e.g. on acceptance of the order (bei Annahme des Auftrags), on delivery of the goods (bei Lieferung der Waren), or on payment of the invoice (bei Zahlung der Rechnung).

(d) When commission payments are due (wann Provisionszahlungen fällig sind), e.g. quarterly (vierteljährlich) or half-yearly (halbjährlich).

(e) The currency in which the commission will be calculated and paid (die Währung in welcher die Provision berechnet und bezahlt wird).

(f) If the agency is exclusive (eine Alleinvertretung), the contract should state to what extent the agent has a right to commission on sales in which he has taken no part (an denen er nicht beteiligt war).

(g) Whether commission is payable on orders placed in the territory (Bezirk) for delivery to a third country or on orders emanating from a third country as a result of canvassing (Kundenbesuche) undertaken by the agent in his territory.

(h) The effect on the commission of subsequent events (nachfolgende Ereignisse), such as cancellation of an order (Auftragsstreichung), price reduction (Preissenkung), etc.

2.9 *The Role of the Agent in the Sales Contract* (*Die Rolle des Handelsvertreters im Verkaufsvertrag*)
Whether the agent buys and resells for his own account (auf eigene Rechnung) or whether he is only an intermediary (ein Vermittler), placing orders with his principal and leaving the latter to invoice clients direct. Whether he guarantees payment of his principal's invoices to his clients, i.e. whether he is a 'del credere' (Delkredere) agent.

2.10 *Terms of Payment* (*Zahlungsbedingungen*)
If the agent is buying and selling on his own account (auf eigene Rechnung) the terms of payment should be agreed, e.g. quarterly credit (vierteljährlicher Abschluss).

2.11 *Quoting Prices* (*Preisangebote*)
How prices are to be quoted (wie Preise angeboten werden sollten), e.g. C.I.F. Hamburg; in DM; etc.

2.12 *Duration and Termination* (*Dauer und Kündigung*)
The contract can be made for an indefinite period (auf unbestimmte Dauer) or for a fixed period (bestimmte Dauer). In the former case, it should be stated that the contract can be determined (gekündigt) by agreed notice (Kündigungsfrist). In the latter case the period must be stated. A trial period (eine Probezeit) can be arranged, during which the contract can be determined without notice (ohne Kündigungsfrist). It may be agreed that certain events (gewisse Vorkommnisse) such as bankruptcy (Bankrott), winding-up by a court order (gerichtliche Liquidation), amalgamation (Fusion) or death (Tod) may entail cancellation without notice (ohne Kündigung/ohne Einhaltung der Kündigungsfrist). Non-performance (Nichterfüllung) of any of the conditions of the contract may, of course, also be specifically mentioned as giving the right of cancellation.

2.13 *Jurisdiction and Arbitration* (*Gerichtsstand und Schiedsgerichtsbarkeit*)
The contract should state the law governing the contract (das für den Vertrag geltende Recht) and the manner in which disputes (Streite) are to be settled. This can be done through a court of law (ein Gericht) or a court of arbitration (ein Schiedsgericht) in one of the countries concerned.

3. A typical Agency Contract

(*englisch-deutsch*)

1. Messrs.: .... (principal) of .... entrust Messrs.: .... (manufacturers' agent) of .... with their <u>sole agency</u> for the territory .... with the sale of the following products:	1. Die Firma .... (vertretene Firma) in .... betraut die Firma .... (Handelsvertreter) in .... mit ihrer Alleinvertretung für den Bezirk .... zum Verkauf folgender Waren: ....

2. The agent <u>will take pains to conduct transactions</u> for the principal and is <u>bound to serve the interests</u> of the <u>principal to the best of his ability.</u> He will do his best <u>to provide all information necessary for the purpose of promoting business,</u> and especially inform the principal immediately about every order received. <u>He may not deviate from the prices, conditions of delivery and payment</u> of the principal <u>without his consent.</u>

2. Der Handelsvertreter hat sich um die Vermittlung von Geschäften zu bemühen und ist verpflichtet, hierbei das Interesse der vertretenen Firma mit der Sorgfalt eines ordentlichen Kaufmannes zu wahren. Er wird der vertretenen Firma nach besten Kräften alle für die Förderung des Geschäftes erforderlichen Nachrichten geben, namentlich ihr von jedem Auftrag unverzüglich Mitteilung machen. Er darf nicht von den Preisen sowie Lieferungs- und Zahlungsbedingungen der vertretenen Firma abweichen.

3. <u>The principal will provide the agent with all necessary samples</u> and with <u>advertising matter free of charge, duties,</u> and <u>carriage. The samples</u>

3. Die vertretene Firma wird dem Handelsvertreter Proben, Muster, Drucksachen, Werbematerial usw. in ausreichender Menge ohne Berechnung

remain the property of the principal, if they are not intended for consumption, and will be returned by the agent on request and at the expense of the principal.

The principal will supply the agent currently with all information of importance for conducting transactions, furthermore he will inform him without delay especially about the acceptance or refusal of orders. He will also inform the agent, if there is a possibility that he can only accept orders to a limited extent.

The agent will be supplied with copies of correspondence with firms in his territory and of all invoices.

4. The agent is only entitled to collect money from the customers in the case of express authorisation.

5. The commission will be .... %

(in letters ....

............................)

....

....

....

....

....

....

of the invoice amount for all transactions, direct and indirect, carried out with customers in the territory mentioned under no. 1.

The principal will furnish the agent

sowie zoll- und frachtfrei zur Verfügung stellen. Die Gegenstände bleiben, soweit sie nicht zum Verbrauch bestimmt sind, Eigentum der vertretenen Firma und werden auf deren Wunsch und ihre Kosten vom Handelsvertreter zurückgesandt.

Die vertretene Firma wird dem Handelsvertreter alle für den Verkauf wichtigen Informationen laufend übermitteln, ihm ferner insbesondere die Annahme oder Ablehnung eines Auftrages unverzüglich mitteilen. Sie wird den Handelsvertreter auch unterrichten, wenn sie Aufträge voraussichtlich nur in begrenztem Umfang annehmen kann.

Von dem Schriftwechsel mit Firmen seines Bezirks und von den Rechnungen erhält der Handelsvertreter Kopien.

4. Der Handelsvertreter ist zum Inkasso von Kundengeldern nur berechtigt, wenn er von der vertretenen Firma dazu ausdrücklich bevollmächtigt ist.

5. Die Provision beträgt .... %

(in Worten ....

............................)

....

....

....

....

....

....

vom Rechnungsbetrag für alle direkten und indirekten Geschäfte, die mit Abnehmern des in Ziffer 1 angegebenen Bezirks abgeschlossen worden sind.

Die vertretene Firma erteilt dem

with a statement of commission due for all deliveries made during the month/quarter of the year not later than the 15th of the following month. This commission, to which according to such statement the agent is entitled, falls due on the day the statement is forwarded.

The agent's claim for commission expires only in respect of any delivery for which it is certain that the customer will not pay; commission that has already been received must be repaid.

The agent is also entitled to commission if it is certain that the principal has not carried out the transactions or not completed them as agreed, unless the principal can prove he is not responsible.

6. The principal will reimburse the agent for the following expenses:

 . . . .
 . . . .
 . . . .
 . . . .

7. The contract shall come into force on the . . . . and is for an indefinite period/for a period of . . . . years.

8. This agreement can be terminated by either party thereto giving . . . . months notice, given by registered letter. Should the contract have been concluded for a definite period, then it shall be prolonged automatically for a further like period provided that notice of termination has not been given within the agreed time to take effect at the end of the period contracted for.

Handelsvertreter für jeden Kalendermonat/jedes Kalendervierteljahr, spätestens bis zum 15. des folgenden Monats, eine Provisionsabrechnung über die in dem Kalendermonat/Kalendervierteljahr erfolgten Lieferungen. Der hiernach dem Handelsvertreter zustehende Provisionsbetrag ist mit der Abrechnung zahlbar.

Der Anspruch auf Provision entfällt nur bezüglich der Lieferungen, von denen feststeht, daß der Kunde sie nicht zahlt; Beträge, die der Handelsvertreter bereits empfangen hat, werden bei der nächsten Provisionsabrechnung angerechnet.

Die Provision ist auch zu zahlen, wenn das Geschäft nicht oder nicht so ausgeführt wird, wie es abgeschlossen worden ist. Dies gilt jedoch dann nicht, wenn die vertretene Firma nachweisen kann, daß sie insoweit kein Verschulden trifft.

6. Die vertretene Firma vergütet dem Handelsvertreter folgende Unkosten:

 . . . .
 . . . .
 . . . .
 . . . .

7. Der Vertrag tritt am . . . . in Kraft und ist auf unbestimmte Dauer/auf die Dauer von . . . . Jahren abgeschlossen.

8. Dieser Vertrag kann von jedem Vertragspartner unter Einhaltung einer Kündigungsfrist von . . . . . Monaten durch eingeschriebenen Brief gekündigt werden. Ist der Vertrag für eine bestimmte Dauer abgeschlossen, so verlängert er sich für den gleichen Zeitraum, wenn er nicht zum Ende der Vertragsdauer mit der vereinbarten Frist gekündigt wird.

9. In other respects the <u>law valid at the seat</u> of the agent <u>is applicable to</u> this agreement.	9. Maßgebend für das Vertragsverhältnis ist im übrigen das am Sitz des Handelsvertreters geltende Recht.
10. <u>Amendments</u> and <u>supplements</u> of this contract <u>must be confirmed in writing.</u>	10. Änderungen und Ergänzungen des Vertrages bedürfen zu ihrer Rechtswirksamkeit der schriftlichen Bestätigung.

....
....
....
....
....
....

Place: .... Date: ....   Ort: .... Datum: ....
....

(Signature of principal)   (Signature of agent)
(Unterschrift des vertretenen Unternehmers)   (Unterschrift des Handelsvertreters)

Letters regarding an Agency

1. Your name has been given to us by the British Embassy in Bonn, which has informed us that you are interested in <u>taking on the representation of foreign firms</u>. We would like to discuss the possibility of an agency with you.

   Die britische Botschaft in Bonn teilt uns mit, dass Sie Vertretungen ausländischer Firmen aufnehmen möchten. Wir sind gerne bereit die Möglichkeit einer Agentur für uns in Deutschland zu <u>besprechen.</u>

2. <u>Kindly let us have full details of</u> your <u>previous experience in this field</u> and also <u>trade references.</u>

   Bitte lassen Sie uns weitere Einzelheiten über Ihre bisherigen Erfahrungen in dieser Branche, sowie <u>Geschäftsreferenzen, zukommen.</u>

3. <u>We have set out our arrangements</u> in a <u>formal agreement</u> which we are enclosing, signed, with this letter. If the <u>terms of this agreement meet with your approval,</u> we should be glad if you would return one copy <u>duly signed</u> to us.

   Wir haben unsere <u>Abmachungen</u> in Form eines Vertrages <u>niedergelegt,</u> den wir mit unserer Unterschrift versehen beilegen. Wenn Sie mit dem Wortlaut dieses Vertrages <u>einverstanden sind,</u> bitten wir um <u>Rücksendung</u> eines von Ihnen unterschriebenen Exemplars.

4. We should like to know on what terms you would be willing to represent us, also the terms on which business is generally conducted in your country.

Wir bitten uns mitzuteilen, unter welchen Bedingungen Sie bereit wären, unsere Vertretung zu übernehmen und uns auch die bei Ihnen im Geschäftsbereich allgemein üblichen Bedingungen anzugeben.

8

Die Absatzwege

BAXTER: Ich wäre Ihnen sehr dankbar, Herr Withof, wenn Sie mir einen Überblick über die _Absatzwege_[1] in der Bundesrepublik geben könnten.
WITHOF: Gerne, Herr Baxter. Zunächst müssen Sie davon ausgehen, dass bei uns der Einkauf sehr zentralisiert ist. Es gibt viele grosse Einkaufszentralen und _Einkaufsverbände_. Im Einzelhandel verlieren die kleinen Händler an Boden. Bei den grossen Unternehmen, zum Beispiel Kaufhäusern, S.B.-Warenhäusern und Versandhäusern steigt der Umsatz laufend.
BAXTER: S.B.-Warenhäuser—was heisst S.B.?
WITHOF: Das sind _Selbstbedienungs-Warenhäuser_. Was Sie—und wir auch, manchmal—'Cash and Carry' Läden nennen. Grundsätzlich gibt es bei uns fünf _Absatzwege_:[2] Erstens die _Versandhäuser_,[2.1] zweitens die _Kaufhäuser, Kaufhausverbände_ und _Kettenläden_,[2.2] drittens die _Einkaufszentralen_ und die _Einkaufsgenossenschaften_,[2.3] und viertens die _S.B.-Warenhäuser_,[2.4] die ich gerade erwähnt habe, und die Verbrauchermärkte.
BAXTER: Und fünftens?
WITHOF: Oh ja, die selbständigen Einzelhändler[2.5]—die sind immer noch sehr wichtig. Besonders für Sie!
BAXTER: Was wäre also der beste Weg für uns?
WITHOF: Das ist schwer zu sagen.... Wir könnten es eventuell mit einem Versandhaus versuchen. Es gibt mehrere die auch mit _Einzelhandelsgeschäften_ zusammenarbeiten. Und das Warenangebot ist sehr gross. Aber ich glaube, ein Kaufhaus wäre besser—oder aber eine Einkaufszentrale.
BAXTER: Ist die Konkurrenz nicht sehr hart?
WITHOF: Gewiss, aber die Umsatzmöglichkeiten sind entsprechend grösser. Wenn wir zum Beispiel nur einen Auftrag von einer Einkaufsgenossenschaft oder freiwilligen Kette bekommen könnten....

Mr Baxter continues his discussion with Herr Withof of Scheerer Elektro-Geräte. He asks him about <u>distribution channels</u> in Germany and Herr Withof explains that there are five main channels. These are <u>mail order houses, large stores, central buying organisations, cash-and-carry stores</u> and <u>independent shops</u>. Mr Baxter asks some questions about the <u>sales management</u> of Scheerer Elektro-Geräte and about <u>sales promotion</u>.

BAXTER: Ja, aber ein solcher Absatzweg wäre vielleicht nicht allzu günstig für unser 'Image' ... Sie haben S.B.-Warenhäuser und Verbrauchermärkte erwähnt. ... Was ist eigentlich der Unterschied?

WITHOF: Der ist nicht sehr gross. Beide haben <u>Verkaufsflächen</u> von mindestens 1000 Quadratmeter. Bei den S.B.-Warenhäusern ist das <u>Sortiment</u> etwas breiter. Man kann dort auch grössere Objekte, wie zum Beispiel Möbel, kaufen.

BAXTER: Meiner Meinung nach wäre es vielleicht vernünftiger mit den selbstständigen Läden anzufangen. Es wird gewiss noch viele Einzelhändler für <u>Elektrogeräte</u> geben, oder nicht?

WITHOF: Ja, sicher, es gibt solche Läden. Und die führen wohl auch Heizlüfter. Nur wäre der Umsatz relativ gering.

BAXTER: Das ist am Anfang weniger wichtig, Herr Withof. Die Hauptsache ist, überhaupt <u>im deutschen Markt Fuss zu fassen.</u>

WITHOF: Das stimmt allerdings! Sie könnten sehr wohl recht haben und der <u>Kundendienst</u> wäre sicherlich leichter zu organisieren. Aber die Anzahl der <u>Vertreterbesuche</u> wäre dementsprechend höher, wenigstens am Anfang.

BAXTER: Wieviele <u>Vertreter</u>$^{(3.2)}$ haben Sie denn, Herr Withof?

WITHOF: Wir haben fünf. Und einen <u>Verkaufsingenieur</u>.

BAXTER: Haben Sie auch einen <u>Gebietsleiter</u>?

WITHOF: Ja, das ist Herr Seefeld. Er ist für den <u>Verkaufsplan</u>,$^{(3.1)}$ den <u>Vertriebskostenplan</u>, die <u>Ausbildung der Vertreter</u>, die <u>Verkaufsüberwachung</u> und die <u>Einhaltung der Quoten</u> usw. verantwortlich.

BAXTER: Gut. Ich möchte ihn gerne kennenlernen. Wir könnten auch die <u>Verkaufsförderung</u>$^{(4)}$ besprechen.

WITHOF: Sie meinen am <u>Verkaufsort</u>?

BAXTER: Ja. Ich habe da einige Vorschläge zu machen in Bezug auf die <u>Schulung des Verkaufspersonals</u>, die <u>Gestaltung von Schaufenstern</u>$^{(4)}$ und dergleichen. Und wir müssen natürlich auch über die <u>Werbung</u> sprechen.

Vocabulary

die Absatzfähigkeit: marketability
das Absatzgebiet: outlet, marketing area
absetzen: to sell or distribute
der Abteilungsleiter: department manager
der Abzahlungskauf: hire purchase
das Angebot: offer, selection (of goods)
das preisgünstige Angebot: special offer
das kombinierte Angebot: combined offer
der Anreiz: incentive
das Anzeigenklischee: advertising block
das Anzeigenmaterial: advertising copy
der Aufkleber: adhesive label
der Aufsteller: display board
die Ausbildung: training
ausstellen: to display
die Ausstellungsfläche: display area

der Blickfang: eye-catcher/advertising stunt

(der) Cash-and-Carry Betrieb (C. & C. Betrieb): cash and carry
der Coupon: coupon

das Diskonthaus: discount house
das Display-Material: display material

der zentrale Einkauf: central buying
die Einkaufsgenossenschaft: co-operative buying association
die zentrale Einkaufsorganisation: central buying organisation
der Einkaufsverband: purchasing group
die Einkaufszentrale: central buying organisation
einlösen: to cash in (a coupon, etc.)
das Einzelhandelsgeschäft: retail shop
der Einzelhändler: retailer
das Entgelt: remuneration
die Entlohnung: remuneration
die Expansion: expansion

das Fachgeschäft: specialist shop
der Filialbetrieb: branch shop
die Filiale: branch shop
die Fixkosten: fixed expenses
das Flugblatt: handbill/leaflet

der Gebietsleiter: area manager
der Geldbetrag: cash
das Gemischtwarengeschäft: general store
das Geschäftsjahr: trading year
der Geschenkartikel: gift
die Geschmacksrichtung: taste (in fashion, etc.)
die Gestaltung: arrangement
das Gestell: rack
die Grosseinkaufsgenossenschaft (G.E.G.): bulk-buying co-operative
der Grosshändler: wholesaler
der Gutschein: coupon, voucher

die Handelsspanne: profit margin
handhaben: to handle
der Händler: tradesman, trader, dealer
die Hausmarke: own brand

das Image: image
der Inlandsmarkt: home market
die Inzahlungnahme: trade-in
die Ist-Zahl: actual figure

der Katalog: catalogue
die freiwillige Kette: voluntary chain (of shops)
der Kettenladen: chain store
das Kettenladenunternehmen: chain store business
die Konsumgenossenschaft: co-operative society
der Konsumverein: co-operative society
die Kosten (plur.): costs
variable Kosten: variable costs
der Kramladen: junk shop
das Kredithaus: credit house

der Laden: shop
die Ladentischauslage: counter display
das Lager: store
auf Lager halten: to keep in store
die Lagerhaltung: storage
der Lagerumsatz: stock turnover

die Markentreue: brand loyalty
der Markt: market
heimischer Markt: home market

der Mehrfarbendruck: colour print
der Mengeneinkauf: bulk purchase
der Mengenrabatt: quantity discount
das Merchandising: merchandising
die unsaubere Methode: unethical method
der Mitarbeiterstab: team of colleagues

das Pappmännchen: cardboard figure
das Plakat: poster
die Prämie: bonus
das Preisausschreiben: competition (with prizes)
die Preislage: price range
der Preisnachlass: price reduction
die Preisskala: price range
das Prospektmaterial: advertising copy

die Quote: quota

der Rabatt: discount, rebate
das Rechnungsjahr: financial year

der Sammeleinkauf: group buying
der Sammelgutschein: voucher (for collecting)
die Sammellieferung: bulk delivery
das Schaufenster: shop window
die Schleichwerbung: covert advertising (editorials, etc.)
die Schulung: training
der Selbstbedienungsladen (S.B.-Laden): self-service shop
das Selbstbedienungswarenhaus: self-service warehouse
selbständig: independent
die Soll-Vorgabe: budgeted target
die Sollzahl: forecast figure
das Sonderangebot: special offer
das Sortiment: assortment, collection, range of goods
das Sortimentgeschäft: general store
das Spezialgeschäft: specialist shop

der Ständer: stand
der Supermarkt: supermarket

die Teilzahlungsrate: instalment
die Tendenz: tendency
die Trödelbude: junk shop, old clothes shop

der Verbrauchermarkt: retail cash and carry store
verbreiten: distribute, circulate (catalogues)
das Verbreitungsgebiet: distribution area
die Verkaufsfläche: sales area
die Verkaufsförderung: sales promotion
der Verkaufsingenieur: sales engineer
die Verkaufsleitung: sales management
das Verkaufspersonal: sales personnel
der Verkaufsplan: sales budget
das Verkaufsteam: sales team
die Verkaufsvoraussage: sales forecast
verpacken: to pack
die Verpackung: packing, wrapping
die Verkaufsunterstützung: merchandising
das Versandgeschäft: mail order business
das Versandhaus: mail order business
verteilen: to distribute
vertreiben: to sell, distribute
vertreten: to represent (a firm)
der Vertrieb: sale, distribution
der Vertriebskostenplan: forecast of marketing costs
die Vorführung: demonstration (of an article)

das Warenhaus: store, large shop
die Warenprobe: sample
die Warenverteilung: distribution of goods
die Werbebotschaft: advertising message

der Zentraleinkauf: central buying

Commercial Notes on Distribution Channels
1. *General*

In Federal Germany there is an established trend towards the concentration (Konzentration) of buyers (Einkäufer) into central purchasing organisations (Einkaufszentralen), groups (Einkaufsverbände) and cooperative buying-associations (Einkaufsgenossenschaften). Central (zentral) and co-operative (genossenschaftlicher) buying (Einkauf) is far more highly developed than in the U.K. Also, in addition to the general increase in retail trade (Einzelhandel), there has been a marked transfer of turnover (Umsatz) from smaller retail outlets (kleinere Einzelhandelsgeschäfte) to larger stores (Kaufhäuser), groups (Verbände) and direct mail organisations (Versandhäuser).

This concentration of buying into tight groups may be considered an obstacle by some exporters, but, if the product is suitable, it can mean that marketing (Absatz) is more convenient and economical. It may be beyond the capacity (Kapazität/Leistungsfähigkeit) of some U.K. manufacturers to supply these major purchasing organisations, but the buyers have to consider regional tastes (örtliche Geschmacksrichtungen) and may consider some products for selected outlets (ausgewählte Absatzgebiete) only.

A small firm with a good, fairly exclusive product, may do better to negotiate (verhandeln) franchise agreements (Alleinverkaufsrechte) with one German distributing firm (Vertriebsunternehmen) than by attempting to supply a bulk market via an intricate breakdown of delivery requirements (spezielle Lieferbedingungen). Although there is a great concentration of buying potential (Einkaufspotential), the large organisations (die grossen Unternehmen) which practise central buying (Zentraleinkauf) are generally not interested in bulk deliveries (Sammellieferungen) to a central warehouse (in ein zentrales Lager). Orders have to be broken down (aufgeteilt) and delivery organised not only to separate areas (Bezirke) of Germany, but to individual towns—even individual stores (Kaufhäuser).

2. Distribution Systems

The channels for buying (Einkauf) and distribution (Verteilung) of consumer goods (Konsumgüter) in Federal Germany fall into the following main groups:

(i) Mail order houses (Versandhäuser).

(ii) Large stores (grosse Kaufhäuser), store groups (Kaufhausverbände) and chains (Kettenladenunternehmen).

(iii) Central and co-operative buying organisations (Einkaufszentralen und Einkaufsgenossenschaften).

(iv) Retail cash-and-carry stores (Verbrauchermärkte oder Selbstbedienungswarenhäuser).

(v) Independent stores and shops (selbstständige Einzelhandelsgeschäfte und Läden).

By far the most important are groups i, ii and iii, but group iv, the cash-and-carry outlet is growing fast.

The trend (der Trend/die Tendenz) for continued increase in turnover (ständige Umsatzsteigerung) for the mail order houses (Versandhäuser), the large stores (Grosskaufhäuser) and groups (Verbände) and the big buying organisations (grosse Einkaufsorganisationen) is well established. All forecasts show that these groups will continue to improve their position (Marktposition verbessern) and further increase their share (Anteil) of the expanding retail trade (erweiternder Einzelhandel).

2.1 *Mail order houses (Versandhäuser oder Versandgeschäfte)*

These have become a very important element (sehr wichtiger Bestandteil) of the distribution system over the past fifteen years. The main companies (die wichtigsten Gesellschaften) handle (führen) a full range of goods (ein vollständiges Sortiment), but there are also many specialist catalogues (Spezialkataloge). Most of the top mail order concerns are associated with (geschäftlich verbunden mit) retail businesses (Einzelhandelsgeschäfte) also engaged in department and chain store activities. This is an important aspect of current development by the mail order companies and in fact the turnover (Umsatz) in the Neckermann stores is now larger than that of their catalogue business (Kataloggeschäft).

There are essential differences (wesentliche Unterschiede) between the direct mail business (Versandgeschäft) in Germany and that in the U.K. In Germany the provision of customer credit (Kundenkredit) is not the main appeal (Anziehungskraft). Most customers pay cash (zahlen bar) on receipt (nach Empfang der Ware).

The agent system (Agentur-System) is very little used. Most of the catalogues (Kataloge) are seen in the customer's own home (zu hause), although some are seen in retail shops (Einzelhandelsläden). For instance some voluntary chain food retailers (freiwillige Lebensmittelketten) show catalogues of mail order houses with which they collaborate (zusammenarbeiten).

Mail order is highly developed (entwickelt) in Germany. Many of the companies circulate their catalogues (verbreiten ihre Kataloge) in the adjoining E.E.C. countries.

The mail order houses now offer a very wide range of goods (haben ein grosses Warenangebot) including expensive items such as real fur coats (echte Pelzmäntel). Their main appeal, however, continues to be their competitive prices (günstige Preise).

There are about 3,000 mail order businesses in West Germany, but the field is dominated by eight large firms, of which the two largest, 'Quelle' and 'Neckermann' account for about a third of the total mail order business.

2.2 *Department stores (Kaufhäuser)*

In the general movement of retail trade (Einzelhandel) from the smaller outlets to the large department stores and store groups, one of the most important areas of expansion (Expansion) has been in foodstuffs (Lebensmittel).

In Germany, as in other countries, the marketing of foodstuffs is moving more and more into department stores (Kaufhäuser), supermarkets (Supermärkte) and cash-and-carry outlets (S.B.-Warenhäuser und Verbrauchermärkte).

The stores carry a far wider price range (Preisskala) than is normally found in U.K. department stores. They sell more on variety of range offered (weitgestreutes Warensortiment) than on display (Auslage) appeal or brand promotion (Markenwerbung). The four major department store concerns in Western Germany are Rudolf Karstadt A.G., Essen; Kaufhof A.G., Köln; Hertie Waren- und Kaufhaus G.m.b.H. (Gesellschaft mit beschränkter Haftung) Frankfurt am Main und Horten A.G., Düsseldorf. They account for about 7% of total retail sales.

2.3 *Central purchasing organisations (Zentrale Einkaufsorganisationen)*

The system of central purchasing organisations, with co-operatives and voluntary chains (Einkaufsgenossenschaften und freiwillige Ketten) is more widely developed in Federal Germany than in any other country. Joint buying (Gemeinschaftseinkauf) operates for almost every type of product, the areas of most interest to British exporters being foodstuffs (Lebensmittel), hardware (Eisenwaren) and textile goods (Textilwaren).

Like the big store groups, these organisations purchase direct from the manufacturers (Hersteller) and are always looking for wider ranges of goods (Warensortimente). Also, like the store groups, the central purchasing organisations are increasingly interested in articles (Artikel) to be sold under their own brand names (Hausmarken).

Food purchasing organisations include Edeka Importe G.m.b.H., Hamburg (39,000 retailers), Rewe-Zentrale G.m.b.H., Köln (12,000 retailers), G.E.G. Grosseinkaufsgenossenschaft Deutscher Konsumgenossenschaften G.m.b.H., Hamburg (with 6,000 retailers) and Handelshof Spar G.m.b.H., Frankfurt/Main (11,700 retailers).

General buying organisations include the Kaufring G.m.b.H., Düsseldorf (584 outlets) and Grohag G.m.b.H., Wiesbaden (532 retailers in Western Germany and 29 in other countries).

2.4 *Cash-and-carry stores* (*Verbrauchermärkte oder Selbstbedienungswarenhäuser*)
These are large self-service shopping centres, situated away from the main city centres. They have a sales area (Verkaufsfläche) of at least 1000 sq m and most of them have large car parks (Parkplätze), as they cater for customers with their own transport. A 'Verbrauchermarkt' offers a wide selection (ein breites Sortiment) of food and non-food products. An 'S.B.-Warenhaus' offers in addition bulky items (Grossobjekte) such as furniture (Möbel) and other fittings (Einrichtungsgegenstände).

The larger cash-and-carry stores are virtually a complete shopping centre (Einkaufszentrum) under one roof. Although there is almost no service (Bedienung) and the absolute minimum of comfort (Komfort) and décor, the stocks include quite good-class furniture (Möbel von recht guter Qualität), expensive foods and drinks and some fashion garments (Modeartikel).

In 1970 there were some 600 of these stores, with a total sales area of 2,371,000 sq m.

2.5 *Smaller, independent shops* (*Kleinere, selbständige Geschäfte/Läden*)
These still represent an important market for the British exporter. Many of these shops specialise in high quality merchandise (sich auf Waren von hoher Qualität spezialisieren) where the British tag (Etikett) can be an advantage. They cater for customers to whom design and good workmanship (Ausführung und gute Qualitätsarbeit) is more important than price. These shops buy individually and are generally not interested in merchandise handled by wholesalers (Grosshändler) or sold by large stores (Kaufhäuser). In the fashion trade (Modesektor) these shops are often called boutiques (Boutique). For many U.K. manufacturers they provide the only outlets (Absatzwege) in Germany. Frequently exclusivity (alleiniges Verkaufsrecht) for a particular town or area is required.

3. *Sales management*

The term sales management (Verkaufsleitung) covers the following functions:

3.1 Preparing the sales budget (Verkaufsplan) for each trading year (Geschäftsjahr). This involves the preparation of a sales forecast

Details of turnover in the various distribution channels mentioned above, together with the names and addresses of the leading firms in each branch, are given in a booklet entitled: 'Selling Consumer Goods to Western Germany' (B.N.E.C. 1970). Useful information is also given about the form which quotations should take (e.g. in DM, C.I.F. Hamburg, etc). Commercial Notes 1 and 2 of this Chapter are based on information contained in this booklet.

(Verkaufsvoraussage). The latter can best be achieved by combining a forecast of sales by each representative with a forecast of sales by product (Absatz nach Artikeln). The gross profit margin (die Brutto-Gewinnspanne) calculated as a percentage of the sales figures (Umsatz) will include a proportion for expenses (Spesen). This will enable the forecast of expenses (Vertriebskostenplan) to be prepared, including fixed expenses (Fixkosten) and variable expenses (variable Kosten).

3.2 *Recruiting and training (Beschaffung und Ausbildung) of management staff (Führungskräfte), representatives (Vertreter) and sales engineers (Verkaufsingenieure)*

The success of a sales team (Verkaufsteam) depends primarily on having a first-class sales manager (Verkaufsleiter) and high-calibre area managers (Gebietsleiter). Training (Ausbildung) of representatives should be both theoretical (theoretisch) and practical (praktisch). It is furthered by sales conferences (Verkaufskonferenzen/Vertretertagungen), lectures with slides (Lichtbildvorträge) and sales bulletins (Verkaufsinformation).

3.3 *Supervising sales (Verkaufsüberwachung/-kontrolle)*

This includes sales analysis (Verkaufsanalyse) on each customer (bei jedem Kunden) and representative (bei jedem Vertreter) with the object of discovering (feststellen/herausfinden) and correcting (richtigstellen) any deviations (Abweichungen) from the plan. Representatives' quotas (Quoten/Soll-Vorgaben) are compared with turnover achieved (werden mit dem tatsächlich erreichten Umsatz verglichen) and a check (Kontrolle) is made on the number of visits (Zahl der Kundenbesuche) which were made and the number of actual sales (Zahl der Verkaufsabschlüsse) compared with the number of their prospective customers (potentielle Kunden).

3.4 *Remuneration (Entgelte)*

This can be a fixed salary (festes Gehalt), commissions (Kommissionsgebühren/Provisionen) payable at a fixed or variable rate (fester oder variabler Satz), bonuses (Prämien) for sales in excess of quotas (Quoten) or a combination of these methods.

4. *Sales promotion (Verkaufsförderung)*

This is the co-ordination of advertising (Werbung) and selling (Verkauf). It is a combination of all the tactical measures (taktische Massnahmen), which serve to open and keep open the channels of distribution (die dem Erschliessen und Offenhalten der Absatzwege dienen). It includes merchandising (Verkaufsunterstützung), i.e. the measures taken to increase retail sales (den Absatz beim Einzelhandel zu steigern).

These measures, which involve the support of the retailer, include the following:

(*a*) Training the retailer's sales staff (Schulung des Verkaufspersonals des Einzelhändlers).

(*b*) Arrangement of shop windows and display areas (Gestaltung von Schaufenstern und Ausstellungsräumen).

(*c*) Grouping and arranging stock (Zusammenfassung und Arrangierung der Sortimente).

(*d*) Special offers (preisgünstige Angebote) to speed stock-turnover (um den Warenumschlag zu beschleunigen).

(*e*) Preparation of advertising aids (Werbemassnahmen) such as advertisements (Anzeigen), display boards (Aufsteller), cardboard figures (Pappmännchen), leaflets (Flugblätter), adhesive labels (Aufkleber), counter displays (Ladentischauslagen), etc., etc.

(*f*) Packaging (Verpackung), including the colouring of the package (Farbe der Verpackung) and its materials.

(*g*) Vouchers or coupons (Gutscheine oder Coupons), for which the customer receives information (Information), samples (Warenproben), gifts (Geschenkartikel) or cash (Bargeld).

(*h*) Preparation of collecting coupons (Sammelgutscheine) used to increase brand-loyalty (Markentreue).

(*i*) Prize competitions (Preisausschreiben).

(*j*) Samples (Warenproben).

(*k*) Combined offers (kombinierte Angebote).

(*l*) Trading-in of old models (Inzahlungnahme von alten Modellen).

(*m*) Credit (Kredit)—usually in the form of hire purchase (Abzahlungskauf); payment is made by instalments (in Teilzahlungsraten).

Letters regarding Visits

1. Our export sales manager, Mr Baxter, will be visiting Düsseldorf next week. He proposes to call on you on the 5th of May at 10.00 a.m., if this is convenient to you.

   Unser Exportleiter, Herr Baxter, wird nächste Woche in Düsseldorf sein. Er beabsichtigt am 5. Mai um 10.00 Uhr bein Ihnen vorzusprechen, wenn es Ihnen recht ist.

2. He will be able to demonstrate our new fan heater.

 Er wird Ihnen unseren neuen Heizlüfter vorführen können.

3. All orders you may give him will receive our immediate and careful attention.

 Alle ihm anvertrauten Bestellungen werden schnell und sorgfältig ausgeführt werden.

9

Die Werbung

WITHOF: Ja, Werbung wird für uns sehr wichtig sein. Ohne Werbung könnten wir kaum vorwärts kommen.

BAXTER: Welche *Medien* würden Sie vorschlagen?

WITHOF: Das ist schwer zu sagen.... Man denkt sofort an *Anzeigenwerbung*.(2) Was aber bei uns nicht das Gleiche wäre wie in England. Wir haben zum Beispiel keine echten überregionalen *Tageszeitungen*,(2.1) abgesehen vielleicht von der 'Bild Zeitung'. Aber in der sind Inserate sehr teuer! Sie müssten also in regionalen *Zeitungen* inserieren. Oder eventuell in *Zeitschriften*(2.2)—etwa im *Stern* oder in der *Quick* oder dergleichen. Die haben einen sehr grossen *Leserkreis*.

BAXTER: So? Was ist denn so ungefähr deren Auflage?

WITHOF: Hmm.... Etwa anderthalb Millionen.

BAXTER: Tatsächlich? Und die Kosten?

WITHOF: Ich weiss nicht genau. Zirka 30 000 Mark pro Seite, soweit ich mich erinnere. Aber es gibt *Mengennachlässe* und *Mal-Nachlässe*.

BAXTER: Wie wäre es mit *Fachzeitschriften*?(2.2)

WITHOF: Um die Einzelhändler zu beeinflussen, meinen Sie? Ja, das sollten wir eigentlich ohnehin tun. Aber es gibt auch noch andere *Werbemittel*. Da ist zum Beispiel die *Kinowerbung*,(5) mit Dias. Sie kann örtlich begrenzt sein und ist verhältnismässig billig.

BAXTER: Ja, und wir könnten Ihnen bei der Anfertigung der Dias behilflich sein. Im Zusammenhang mit einer *Anschlagwerbung*(6.1) in derselben Stadt könnten wir einen sehr wirkungsvollen Werbefeldzug aufziehen.

WITHOF: Ganz gewiss! Und besonders wenn wir dazu auch noch *die Hörfunkwerbung*(3) benutzen.

BAXTER: Ach ja, die hatte ich ganz vergessen. Ich nehme an, dass es hier regionale Sender gibt?

WITHOF: Ja, die gibt es. Da ist zum Beispiel der Westdeutsche Rundfunk; der hat über fünf Millionen Hörer.

BAXTER: Eine sehr grosse Zuhörerschaft, also! Aber Sie haben doch wohl auch *Fernsehwerbung*,(4) nicht wahr?

Mr Baxter discusses with Herr Withof the various advertising media, with a view to deciding on an advertising campaign. Herr Withof points out some of the differences between advertising in Germany and Great Britain and explains the characteristics of the chief media—press, radio, television, posters, cinema, direct mail and exhibitions.

WITHOF: Ja, wir haben zwei Programme die Werbung ausstrahlen. Aber die sind natürlich wahnsinnig teuer und kämen für uns wohl kaum in Frage.
BAXTER: Ja, das glaube ich auch nicht. Aber es gibt wohl noch andere Möglichkeiten auf diesem Gebiet? Wie wäre es mit *Direktwerbung?*[8]
WITHOF: Gewiss, das wäre bestimmt nicht schlecht. Wir haben eine Adressenkartei aller Elektrogeschäfte in unserem Bezirk; denen könnten wir einen Werbebrief und einen Ihrer Prospekte schicken.
BAXTER: Ja, gut. Und wir dürfen die grossen *Ausstellungen*[7] nicht vergessen. Wir haben die Absicht nächstes Jahr auf der Hannover Messe auszustellen.
WITHOF: Ausgezeichnet! Das kann uns nur nützen! Es kommen Interessenten aus der ganzen Bundesrepublik zu dieser Messe.
BAXTER: Ja, ich weiss. Allen unseren Bezirksvertretern wird damit geholfen. Übrigens, können Sie mir eine gute *Werbeagentur*[9] empfehlen?
WITHOF: Ja, das kann ich. Es gibt eine erstklassige Voll-Service Agentur in Düsseldorf. Sie hat eine *Gestaltungsgruppe*,[9.7] eine *Streuungsgruppe* und eine *Marktforschungsgruppe*. Sie heisst Werbeagentur Heinrich Hamacher. Ich kann sie sehr empfehlen.
BAXTER: Vielen Dank. Ich werde sie also betreffend unseres Werbeplans konsultieren und mich auch über eventuelle Marktforschung beraten lassen.

Vocabulary

die Adressenkartei: card index, address list
die Agenturprovision: agency commission
die Anschlagsäule: advertisement pillar
die Anschlagwerbung: poster or outdoor advertising
ansprechen: to appeal to (as advertisement to customer)
die Anzeige: advertisement
die kleine Anzeige (Kleinanzeige): 'classified' advertisements
die Anzeigenhäufigkeit: frequency of insertion
der Anzeigeninhalt: (advertising) copy
der Anzeigenpreis: advertising rate
die Anzeigenpreisliste: advertising card
der Anzeigenraum: advertisement space
der Anzeigentext: (advertising) copy
die Anzeigenwerbung: (print or press) advertising
A.R.D. (Arbeitsgemeinschaft der Rundfunkgesellschaften Deutschlands): 1st TV channel (regional, commercial)
die Auflage (einer Zeitung u.s.w.): circulation (of a newspaper, etc.)
der Auftraggeber: principal
das Auslagefenster: show window
der Ausstellkasten: showcase
der Ausstellungsraum: showroom

die Begutachtung: expert opinion
die Beratung: advice
der Bogen: sheet (of paper)

das Diapositiv: transparency
die Dienstleistung: service
die Direktwerbung: direct mail-advertising
Drittes (III.) Programm: Third T.V. channel (regional, non-commercial)

der Empfang: reception

das Fachblatt/die Fachzeitschrift: specialist periodical, trade journal
der farbige Fernsehspot: colour-T.V. advertisement or spot

die Fernsehwerbung: T.V. advertising
die Forschung: research
die Full-Service Werbeagentur: full-service advertising agency
der Funkspot: radio commercial
der Funktext: radio script

der genehmigte Werbeetat: advertising appropriation or budget
die Gesellschaftszeitschrift: society magazine
die Gestaltung: display, presentation, creative work, arrangement, design
die Gestaltungsgruppe: creative division
die Gestaltungskosten: technical costs
der Goodwill: goodwill of a business
die Grundlage: basis
der Grundpreis: basic price

die Hörfunkwerbung: radio advertising

die aktuelle Illustrierte: topical illustrated magazine
das Inserat: advertisement
die Insertionsgebühr: advertising charge
die institutionelle Werbung: institutional advertising (Prestige)

die Kennziffer: box or code numbers (for adverts)
das Kino: cinema
kleine Anzeigen: classified advertisements
der Klischeefuss: printing block
die Kontaktgruppe: 'account group' (for advertising agency)
der Kontaktor: account executive
der Kunde (voraussichtlich, möglich): customer, client (potential)
der Kundenkreis: clientele, customers

das Layout: layout
die Leinwand: screen
die Leserschaft: readership
der Lesezirkel: reading-circle, magazine library
die Litfasssäule: poster column

das Magazin: magazine
der Mal-Nachlass: quantity rebate
die Markenwerbung: brand advertising
die Marktforschungsgruppe: market research
die Massen-Medien: mass media
der Maueranschlag: wall poster
die Mediaforschung: media research
das Medium (pl. Medien, Media): advertising medium
der Mengennachlass: quantity rebate, reduction
die Millimeterhöhe: millimeter height (of an advertisement) (c.f. column-inch)

der Nachlass: rebate

die Öffentlichkeitsarbeit: public relations work

das Pauschalhonorar: fee or payment
das Plakat: poster
der Platz: position (of an advertisement on page)
die Postversandwerbung: direct mail advertising
die Prestigewerbung: prestige advertising
der Probeabzug: proof (sheet), pull
die Produktionsgruppe: production division
die Programmzeitschrift: programme magazine
die Public-Relations-Gruppe: public relations division

der Rabatt: rebate
der Raum: room or space
die Reichweite: coverage
die Reinzeichnung: final art work
die Reklame: advertising, advertisement, publicity
die Rohskizze: layout
der Rundfunk: radio

das Schlagwort: slogan
der Schriftsatz: composition, type
die Schutzvorrichtung: safeguard
die Seite: page
der Seitenpreis: page rate

der Seitenteil: part page
sittenwidrig: unethical
die Sonntagszeitung: Sunday paper
die Spaltenzahl: number of columns
das Standardformat: standard size
die Stereotypieplatte: 'stereo' or block
die Stosskraft: impact (of an advertisement)
die Streubreite: coverage
streuen: to distribute
die Streukosten: media expenditure, space charge, coverage costs
der Streuplan: space schedule
die Streuplanung: media strategy
die Streuung: media planning, media schedule, coverage
die Streuungsgruppe: media planning division
der Streuweg: media chosen for a campaign

die Tageszeitung: daily paper
die Teilseite: part-page
der Testmarkt: test market
die T.V.-Werbung: T.V. advertising

übertragen: to transmit
der Umsatz: turnover or 'billing'

verrufen: to decry
die Vertrauenswerbung: public relations
die Voll-Service Werbeagentur: full service advertising agency
die Vorführung: performance
die Vorskizze (rohe): (rough) draft layout

die Werbeagentur: advertising agency
der Werbeanspruch (übertriebene): claim (sweeping)
die Werbeaktion: advertising campaign
der Werbeblock: advertising periods (T.V.)
der Werbebrief: sales letter
die Werbeerfolgskontrolle: checking on advertising success, keying
der Werbeetat: advertising budget
der Werbefachmann: advertising expert or advertising man
der Werbefeldzug: advertising campaign

der Werbefunk: radio advertising
der Werbegemeinte: advertising target
die Werbekampagne: advertising campaign
die Werbekonzeption: advertising concept
die Werbekosten: advertising costs
der Werbekostenplan: advertising budget
der Werbeleiter: advertising manager
die Werbemassnahmen: advertising measures
das Werbemittel: advertising medium or media (general sense)
die Werbemittelforschung: media research
werben (er wirbt): to advertise (he advertises)
der Werbeplan: advertising budget
das Werbeschild: sign board
die Werbesendung: advertising broadcast ('commercial' on radio or T.V.)
die Werbeszene: 'commercial' (T.V.)
der Werbeträger: advertising medium (specific), the means by which contact is made between the public and the general media; examples are newspapers, magazines, etc.
das Werbeziel: advertising target
die Werbung in Filmtheatern: cinema advertising
die Werbung in Verkehrsmitteln: advertising in public transport
die Werbung um öffentliches Vertrauen: public relations
der Werbungstreibende: advertiser

der Zeilenpreis: price per line
die Zeitschrift: magazine
die Zeitung: newspaper
die Zielgruppe: target group
Zweites Deutsches Fernsehen (2.DF): second German T.V. Channel (national, commercial)

Commercial Notes on Advertising Media

1. *The principal media* (*Werbemittel oder Medien*)

Approximate percentage share of advertising billings (ungefährer Anteil am Brutto-Werbeumsatz) in Federal Germany are as follows:

Press Advertising (Anzeigenwerbung)

Newspapers (Zeitungen)	33,7%
Magazines (Zeitschriften)	19,5%
Radio Advertising (Hörfunkwerbung)	2,1%
Television Advertising (Fernsehwerbung)	7,1%
Poster Advertising (Anschlagwerbung)	2,9%
Address Book Advertising (Adressbücher)	1,6%
Cinema Advertising (Werbung im Filmtheater)	0,7%
Direct Mail Advertising (Direktwerbung)	32,4%
	100,0%*

*From 'This is your German Market', published by Axel Springer Verlag and Z.A.W., Bonn.

In 1972 this 100% equalled DM 8,139 million. In addition, and not included in the above figures, there is advertising by means of trade fairs and exhibitions (Messen und Ausstellungen).

2. Press advertising (Anzeigenwerbung)

2.1 Newspapers (Zeitungen)

There are no national newspapers in Germany really similar to the British national dailies, although the 'Bild-Zeitung' with daily net sales (tägliche Verkaufsauflage) of over 3,7 million, is in a class by itself. It covers the whole country, but has local editions (Lokalausgaben) for Munich (München), Hamburg, Frankfurt/Main, Hanover [Hannover], Berlin, Cologne [Köln], Essen and Stuttgart. These offer facilities for regional advertising.

Daily newspapers (Tageszeitungen) have a regional coverage (regionale Reichweite) but some, such as 'Die Welt' (0.31 m circulation), 'Handelsblatt' (0.09 m) and 'Frankfurter Allgemeine' (0.38 m) have a considerable readership (Leserkreis) throughout the whole Federal Republic among people of a high and influential social rating.

There are 146 independent daily newspapers (Tageszeitungen) with a total circulation (Auflage) of about 25 million. The circulation of daily papers has lost ground to the ever-growing national periodicals and the daily paper has therefore diminished a little in value to the advertisers (Werbungstreibende). In general, the papers with a circulation wider than the mere regional, can be classed as good media (Werbeträger) for all kinds of prestige advertising (institutionelle) and public relations (Vertrauenswerbung/P.R.), whilst regional papers are good media when advertising in a market in a particular area (Bezirk), in a test market (Testmarkt), or in connection with local dealers (Lokalhandel).

Because of the lack of daily newspapers with a high national circulation, magazines (Zeitschriften) have a much greater importance in Germany as a mass medium.

This is increased by the extensive use of magazine libraries (Lesezirkel), of which there are some 600 in the Federal Republic, serving some seven million readers.

2.2 Magazines and periodicals (Magazine und Zeitschriften)

The standard of presentation (Gestaltung) of advertisements (Anzeigen/Inserate) in German magazines is very high. Advertising rates (Anzeigenpreise) vary according to the circulation (Auflage) of the journal.

There are about 230 'consumer magazines'; some of the main ones with an approximate circulation (1973) as follows:

Illustrated news magazines* (*Aktuelle Illustrierte*):

	million
'Quick'	1,3
'Neue Revue'	1,4
'Der Stern'	1,6
'Bunte Illustrierte'	1,6

Programme-periodicals (*Programm-Zeitschriften*)

	million
'Hör Zu'	3,5
'TV Hören und Sehen'	2,1
'Funk Uhr'	1,5

Women's, film and fashion magazines (*Frauen-, Film-, und Modezeitschriften*)

	million
'Burda-Moden'	1,7
'Für Sie'	1,1
'Brigitte'	1,4

Other papers and periodicals (*andere Zeitungen und Zeitschriften*)
This group includes such periodicals as 'Das Beste aus Reader's Digest' (1,2 million net sales), 'Der Spiegel' (0,9) and a group of magazines classed as the 'society press' (Gesellschafts-Zeitschriften), like 'Chic' (0,08). A publication after the style of the British Consumer's Research magazine 'Which?' is called 'D-Mark'.

2.3 *Cost of press advertising* (*Anzeigenwerbung*)
The basis (Grundlage) for calculating the price of an advertisement is the rate-card (Anzeigenpreisliste), which shows the basic price (Grundpreis). Space (Anzeigenraum) is quoted either by 'millimeter depth' (Millimeterhöhe) and number of columns (Spaltenzahl) or by the page (Seite) and part-page (Seitenteil). A discount (Rabatt) is usually given for advertisements repeated several times (mehrfach) in a year (während des Jahres). This is calculated either on the total volume, in which case

---

*Annual and quarterly reports giving details of circulation (Auflage) and readership (Leserkreis) of these magazines are issued by: 'I.V.W.' (Informationsgemeinschaft zur Feststellung der Verbreitung von Werbeträgern e.V.), 5320 *Bad Godesberg*, Kölnerstrasse 107b.

it is known as a 'Mengennachlass' or on the number of advertisements, when it is known as a 'Mal-Nachlass'. The two most important aspects of an advertisement are the position (Platz) and the design (die Gestaltung).

3. *Radio advertising (Hörfunk-Werbung)*

   Broadcasting (Rundfunk-Sendung) is carried out on a regional basis, the following being the principal stations (Sender): (the approximate number of radio licences is shown in brackets)

	million
Westdeutscher Rundfunk	5,1
Norddeutscher Rundfunk	3,6
Bayrischer Rundfunk*	3,1
Südwestfunk*	2,0
Süddeutscher Rundfunk*	1,7
Hessischer Rundfunk*	1,6
Sender 'Freies Berlin'*	0,9
Radio Bremen*	0,3
Saarländischer Rundfunk*	0,3

4. *Television advertising (Fernseh- oder T.V.-Werbung)*

   There are three television channels in Federal Germany—A.R.D., Z.D.F. and III. Programm—but only the first two carry advertising.

   The A.R.D. (Arbeitsgemeinschaft der öffentlichrechtlichen Rundfunkanstalten Deutschlands) or First Programme, is broadcast and controlled by the regional stations (Länder-Anstalten). The percentage of licence holders in each transmitting zone and the location of the transmitter are as follows:

WDR	Westdeutscher Rundfunk—Köln	25%
NDR	Norddeutscher Rundfunk—Hamburg	20%
BR	Bayrischer Rundfunk—München	17%
SFB	Sender Freies Berlin—Berlin	8%
HR	Hessischer Rundfunk—Frankfurt	8%
SWF	Südwestfunk—Baden-Baden	8%
SDR	Süddeutscher Rundfunk—Stuttgart	8%
RB	Radio Bremen—Bremen	3%
SR	Saarländischer Rundfunk—Saarbrücken	3%

*Only these stations transmit advertising and they restrict it to certain hours. Radio Luxemburg broadcasts advertising in German throughout the day and covers most of the western part of the Federal Republic.

The Z.D.F. (Zweites Deutsches Fernsehen) is nationwide and has a central administration in Mainz. The III. Program (Drittes Programm) transmits locally from the A.R.D. stations, but does not carry advertising.

Good reception (Empfang) of German programmes is possible in parts of France, Switzerland, Austria, Denmark, Holland and Belgium.

In Germany T.V. advertising is governed by very strict rules which allow no advertising after 8 o'clock, no advertising at all on Sundays and Public Holidays and no advertising in the middle of programmes. There are four advertising periods (Werbeblocks) in an evening, which over the year must average out at not more than 20 minutes a day and are clearly separated off from the programme output. The preparation of advertisements and the booking of transmission time (Fernsehübertragung) is invariably left to an advertising agency (Werbeagentur). The cost of a colour-T.V. 'spot' (Farbfernseh-Spot) or a black-and-white spot (schwarz-weiss Spot) varies considerably between stations. One minute on the biggest network, WDR, costs DM 24,200 (1972).

5. *Cinema advertising (Kinowerbung)*

Although cinemas (Kinos) have lost ground considerably in competition with television, the screen (Leinwand) is still a medium (Werbeträger) of considerable importance, especially for local publicity (örtlich begrenzte Werbung) when slides (Diapositive) are commonly used.

Publicity films (Reklamefilme) average 2 minutes in length and are 66 metres long. There is a restriction (Beschränkung) to 200 metres (or 6 minutes) on the amount of publicity film that may be shown at any one performance (eine Filmvorstellung).

Animated cartoon films (Zeichentrickfilme) are normally in lengths of 6, 12 or 14 metres and are used extensively by advertisers.

6. *Other advertising media*

6.1 *Poster advertising (Anschlagwerbung)*

There are poster columns (Litfass-Säulen/Anschlagesäulen) in all towns and nearly all villages throughout the Federal Republic. Space (Anzeigenraum) is sold by special agents, of whom there are more than 200 working closely with advertising agencies.

The standard sizes (Standardformate) for posters (Plakate) conform with German Industrial Standard DIN 683 and are based on size A1, a whole sheet (ganzer Bogen) measuring 84 × 95 cm.

6.2 *Transport Advertising (Werbung durch Verkehrsmittel)*

There are over 7,000 railway stations (Bahnhöfe) in Western Germany, 37 of which are main stations (Hauptbahnhöfe). Media available include wall posters (Maueranschläge), sign boards (Plakatschilder), showcases (Ausstellkästen) and display windows (Schaufenster). Posters of standard size (Plakate von normaler Grösse) can be seen on hoardings (Plakatflächen) and advertisement pillars (Plakatsäulen/ Litfass-Säulen). Advertisements can also be displayed in railway carriages (Eisenbahnwagen) or in rail-buses (Bahn-Busse), belonging to the German State Railway (Deutsche Bundesbahn). The same applies to buses (Omnibusse) belonging to the post office (Deutsche Bundespost) and to trams (Strassenbahnen), which run in the major cities. These vehicles also display advertising material on their bodywork (Karosserie).

All advertising is subject to certain ethical considerations (ethische Erwägungen). Advertisers (Werbetreibende) are not allowed to decry (herabsetzen/verleumden) the wares of their competitors (Konkurrenten), either directly or by implication. Exaggerated claims (übertriebene Behauptungen/Ansprüche), unsupported by professional evidence, are forbidden. There are safeguards (Schutzmassnahmen) against corrupting influences on youth. These are similar to the controls appertaining to British T.V. advertising.

7. *Trade fairs and exhibitions* (*Messen und Ausstellungen*)
Germans set a high value on fairs and any firm seriously interested in the market should consider participating in one or more of them.

Some fairs, like the Hannover Messe, held annually in April/May, are of a general nature and cover a very wide range of products. Most, however, are specialised. Examples are 'Die Internationale Grüne Woche' in Berlin; ANUGA and INTERZUM, Cologne; IGEDO and INTERPACK in Düsseldorf; INTERSTOFF in Frankfurt; BAUMA and ELECTRONICA in Munich and the Spielwarenmesse (Toyfair) in Nüremberg. The majority of these fairs are international in character and attract buyers from all over the world. Space is limited and has to be booked well in advance. Full details of fairs can be obtained from the Ausstellungs- und Messeausschuss der Deutschen Wirtschaft e.V., 500 Köln, Engelbertsgasse 21A or from the Department of Trade.

8. *Direct mail advertising*
   (*Postversandwerbung/Direktwerbung*)
There are many firms which will provide lists of addresses (Anschriften mittels einer Adressenkartei) or address labels (Aufklebeadressen/ Adress-Schilder) for use in direct mail advertising (Postversandwerbung/Direktwerbung) and envelopes can also be provided for the advertiser who wishes to make a direct approach to the prospective customer (möglicher Kunde). The sales letter (Werbebrief) is the most

important item of any mailing shot which includes leaflets (Prospekte), presents (Werbegeschenke), samples (Muster) or catalogues (Kataloge).

9. *The advertising agency*

A full-service advertising agency (eine Voll-Service oder Full-Service Werbeagentur) offers, as in the U.K. a range of services (Dienstleistungen) which include the following:

9.1 *Advice (Beratung)*

Advice on marketing problems (Warenabsatz-/Marketing Probleme), brand policy (Markenpolitik), sales policy (Verkaufspolitik), merchandising problems (Merchandising-Probleme), advertising policy (Werbepolitik), planning (Planung) of sales seminars (Verkaufstagungen) and preparation of catalogues, sales aids and house magazines (Vorbereitung von Katalogen, Verkaufshilfen und Hauszeitschriften).

9.2 *Research and information (Forschung und Information)*

Carrying out of studies (Durchführung von Studien) and advice on consumer structure and habits (Verbraucherstruktur und -gewohnheiten), the extent and situation (der Umfang und die Lage) of the market, influence of the season (Einfluss der Saison) and economic trends (wirtschaftliche Trends) on sales, pricing (Preisgestaltung).

Opinion research in the retail and wholesale trade (Untersuchung von Einzel- und Grosshändlermeinungen); finding out customer reaction (Verbraucheruntersuchung) to competitors' products (Konkurrenzprodukte).

9.3 *Planning and creative work (Planung und Gestaltung)*

Development (Entwicklung) of new products, preparation of rough sketches or lay-outs (rohe Vorskizzen oder Layouts) for packaging (Verpackung) and preparation of complete packaging designs (fertige Packungsentwürfe); development of basic ideas (tragende Motive) for advertising campaigns (Werbekampagne), advice on the size of the budget (Etat) and its distribution (Aufteilung); determination (Bestimmung) of the national, regional or local field of operation (Einsatzraum) for the campaign; development of complete trade publicity campaigns (Händler-Werbekampagne), complete merchandising-sales programmes (Merchandising/Verkaufsprogramme); assistance with the preparation of exhibition stands (Standgestaltung für Messen).

9.4 *Final art work and production (Reinzeichnung und Produktion)*

Completion (Anfertigung) of detailed layouts (detaillierte Layouts), preparation of prototypes (Prototypen) such as photographs (Fotos), composition (Schriftsatz), blocks (Klischees) for advertisements (Inserate), T.V. advertising (Fernsehwerbung), posters (Plakate).

9.5 *Radio, Film, and T.V. Advertising (Funk-, Film-, und Fernsehwerbung)*
Writing radio scripts (Funktexte) or commercials (Werbeszenen) for the principal (Auftraggeber); supervision (Überwachung) of radio 'spots' (Funkspots); films (Filme) and T.V. 'spots' (Fernsehspots); advising on surveys of T.V. viewers (Begutachtungen von Fernsehzuschauerzahlen).

9.6 *Media Planning (Streuung)*
Carrying out (Durchführung) of research into the readership (Leserschaft) and the quality (Qualität) and coverage (Reichweite) of each of the media employed; preparation of media appropriations (Kostenvoranschläge) and of media schedules (Streupläne), allocation of orders (Auftragsvergabe) to the media (Werbeträger); carrying out negotiations regarding the placing of advertisements (Placierungsverhandlungen) and negotiations over possible rebates or discounts (Rabatte oder Preisnachlässe).

9.7 A full-service agency would normally have some or all of the following divisions:

>Account Division (Kontaktgruppe)
>Creative Division (Gestaltungsgruppe)
>Media Planning Division (Streuungsgruppe)
>Market Research Division (Marktforschungsgruppe)
>Public Relations Division (Public Relations Gruppe)
>Production Division (Produktionsgruppe)

9.8 *Remuneration*
This is usually by commission (Provision) on billings (Umsatz).
Other forms are the service-fee system (das 'amerikanische' oder 'Service-Fee System'), flat-rate payment or fee (Pauschalhonorar), or payment for individual services (Honorierung der Einzelleistungen).

9.9 *Principal agencies operating in Federal Germany*
(by approximate order of billings) include:

>H. V. McCann Company—Frankfurt
>Lintas Werbeagentur—Hamburg
>J. Walter Thompson—Frankfurt
>Werbeagentur Dr Hegemann—Düsseldorf/Ffm.
>Troost Werbeagentur—Düsseldorf
>Young & Rubicam Werbung—Frankfurt
>William Wilken Werbeagentur—Hamburg
>Werbe-Gramm Gesellschaft für Wirtschaftswerbung—Düsseldorf
>Team Werbeagentur—Düsseldorf
>Heumann, Ogilvy & Mather—Frankfurt

10. Linguistic differences

Both German and English are part of the West Germanic group of languages and have many points in common. German shares with English the ability to economise in words by coupling them together, as in: 'Die meistgekaufte Klinge Deutschlands' and 'Weltwunder für Weltbummler'.

However, it is rarely possible to translate a successful English advertising pun or phrase directly into German. There are many pitfalls. For example, the word 'mist' in English, used widely by hairspray manufacturers, means 'manure' in German and the word 'gift', used in gift carton, for example, means 'poison' in German.

It is advisable to leave copywriting for German advertisements to a German advertising agency.

Letters about Advertising. (*To an advertising agency in Germany*)

1. We have recently appointed an agent for the German Federal Republic and intend to carry out some press advertising. Would you please give us your advice as to which newspapers and magazines would be most suitable for this purpose?

    Wir haben kürzlich einen Handelsvertreter in der Deutschen Bundesrepublik engagiert und beabsichtigen einen Anzeigenwerbefeldzug durchzuführen. Würden Sie uns bitte raten, welche Zeitungen bezw. Zeitschriften dafür am geeignetsten wären.

2. Our advertising appropriation would allow us to spend DM ... in your country. Do you think that this amount would be sufficient to book some air time on television, or would you advise us to limit our advertising to radio advertising?

    Unser Werbeetat würde es uns ermöglichen DM ... in Ihrem Lande auszugeben. Glauben Sie, dass dieser Betrag ausreichen würde Fernsehwerbung zu nutzen oder würden Sie uns empfehlen, dass wir uns auf Rundfunkwerbung beschränken.

3. We should be glad to have your opinion on the enclosed layouts.

    Wir wären Ihnen für Ihre Stellungnahme zu beiliegenden Rohskizzen sehr dankbar.

4. We should like the enclosed advertisement to be inserted six times in double column.

    Wir bitten beiliegende Anzeige sechsmal in Dopplespalten zu inserieren.

10

Die Auslandsmarktforschung

BAXTER: Herr Withof, bevor wir mit dem Verkauf unserer Produkte im Bundesgebiet anfangen, sollten wir eigentlich den Markt näher kennen.
  Der Leiter unserer Vertriebsabteilung hätte gern weitere Informationen über die Nachfrage nach Heizlüftern. Er muss seine Verkaufsprognose so bald wie möglich fertigstellen. Könnten Sie mir da helfen?
WITHOF: Aber gerne, Herr Baxter! Was möchten Sie wissen?
BAXTER: Nun, wir haben schon in England etwas 'Schreibtischarbeit' geleistet und durch *indirekte Forschung*[2] haben wir zum Beispiel festgestellt, dass vor zwei Jahren rund 950 000 Heizlüfter in der Bundesrepublik Deutschland hergestellt wurden.
WITHOF: Wirklich? Woher haben Sie denn diese Auskunft?
BAXTER: Aus dem Buch 'Industrie und Handwerk'. Ich glaube es wird vom Kohlhammer Verlag in Mainz herausgebracht.
WITHOF: Ach ja, das stimmt. Sie sind wirklich gut informiert, Herr Baxter.
BAXTER: Hmm.... Man tut was man kann! Wir wissen auch, dass im gleichen Jahr rund 35 000 Heizlüfter importiert und 200 800 exportiert wurden. Das bedeutet, dass ungefähr 784 200 Geräte im Inlandsmarkt verkauft wurden.
WITHOF: Ja, das dürfte wohl stimmen....
BAXTER: Im vergangenen Jahr ist aber der Gesamtverbrauch im Inlandsmarkt um 5% gefallen; wir können somit also im nächsten Jahr mit einem Markt von ungefähr 750 000 Stück rechnen.
WITHOF: Ja, das könnte gut sein.
BAXTER: Daraus ergibt sich, dass wir bei einem halben Prozent Marktanteil in zwei Jahren mit dem Verkauf von....
WITHOF: ... etwa 3,700 Heizlüftern rechnen könnten. Das wäre durchaus möglich.

Mr Baxter finishes his talk with Herr Withof by asking for his help in preparing a sales forecast and in carrying out market research. First they discuss the indirect method of research and the various sources of statistical information available in both countries. Then they discuss the direct method, including a survey of the market by means of interviews and motivation surveys.

BAXTER: Also gut. Wir dürfen aber nicht vergessen, dass unsere Annahmen auf *Sekundärmaterial* beruhen. Wir müssen unbedingt auch noch *Primärdaten*[3.3] erheben. Ich möchte da eine begrenzte *Marktanalyse* vorschlagen.

WITHOF: Wird gemacht! Welche Punkte sollen wir besonders behandeln?

BAXTER: Da gibt es mehrere: zuerst müssen wir einmal feststellen, welche Modelle am meisten gekauft werden. Zum Beispiel welche Leistung und wieviele Heizstufen bevorzugt werden, und aus welchen gründen. Das bedeutet *Motivforschung!*[3.1]

WITHOF: Stimmt. Ich kenne da ein *Forschungsinstitut*[3.2] das solche Untersuchungen durchführt.

BAXTER: Gut. Mit denen könnten wir einen *Fragebogen* besprechen. Die Gruppe der Befragten braucht nicht allzu gross zu sein.

WITHOF: Nein, die Sache wird ohnehin recht teuer. Was möchten Sie sonst noch wissen?

BAXTER: Wir brauchen Auskunft über die *Konkurrenz*. Welche Firmen verkaufen hier? Wie hoch ist deren *Marktanteil?* Was sind ihre normalen *Absatzwege?* Wie *werben* Sie?

WITHOF: Herr Baxter, wir werden Ihnen in jeder Hinsicht behilflich sein! Wir kennen die Konkurrenz nur zu gut!

BAXTER: Das kann ich mir vorstellen! Also, Herr Withof, das wäre wohl alles für heute. Ich bin Ihnen sehr dankbar für Ihre Hilfe.

Vocabulary

der Absatz: sale, marketing, distribution (of goods)
die Absatzforschung: marketing research
die Absatzmethode: marketing method
der Absatzplan: marketing plan
die Absatzprognose: marketing forecast
die Absatzstatistik: marketing statistic
der Absatzweg: distribution channel
die Absatzziffer: sales figure
die 'ad-hoc' Survey: 'ad-hoc' survey
das Angebot: quotation, supply (as in supply and demand)
die Annahme: assumption
die Adressenliste: address list
die Archivalien: records/archive material
das Archivmaterial: records/archive material
der Auftraggeber: principal (e.g. client for whom a research company works)
die Ausfuhrstatistiken: export statistics
die Auslandsmarktforschung: export market research
die Auswertung: evaluation

der Befrager: interviewer
der Befragte: interviewee
die Befragung: interview
die Bevölkerung: population
das Bruttosozialprodukt: gross national product

die Devisenkontrolle: exchange control
die direkte Methode: direct method
der Durchschnitt: average
die Durchschnittsbestimmung: average-analysis
die Durchschnittserhebung: average-analysis

das Einfuhrkontingent: import quota
die Einfuhrlizenz: import licence
die Einfuhrstatistiken: import statistics
die Einkaufsgewohnheit: buying habit
das Einkommen: income
die Enquete: survey, enquiry, poll
die Erhebung: survey
der Erinnerungstest: recall test

die Feldarbeit: field work
die Forschung: research
die qualitative Forschung: qualitative research
die quantitative Forschung: quantitative research
der Fragebogen: questionnaire

die Gesamtmasse: 'universe', population
die Gruppendiskussion: group discussion

das Handelsadressbuch: trade directory
der Haushalt: household
die Haushaltung: household
das Haushaltstagebuch: housekeeping diary

die Indexzahl: index figure
die Informationsquelle: source of information
der Inlandsmarkt: home market
das Interview: interview

die Käuferforschung: customer research
die Kaufkraft: buying power
das Kaufmotiv: buying motive
die Konjunktur: market conditions, state of the economy
die Konkurrenz: competition
die Konsumforschung: consumer research

die Lagerbestandsaufnahme: stock audit
liberalisieren: to liberalise

das Marketing: marketing
die Marktanalyse: market survey, market analysis
die Marktbeobachtung: continuous survey
der Marktforscher: market researcher
die Marktforschung: market research
die Marktuntersuchung: market survey
die charakteristische Marktuntersuchung: controlled sample
die regionale Marktuntersuchung: area sample
die direkte Methode: direct method

die indirekte Methode: indirect method
der Mittelwert: average, mean, median
die Motivforschung: motivational research

die Nachfrage: demand (for goods)
das Nachschlagebuch: reference book

die Primärdaten: primary material
das Primärmaterial: primary material
die Produktforschung: product research
der projektive Test: T.A.T. (thematical Apperceptional Test)
der Prozentanteil: percentage

die qualitative Forschung: qualitative research
die quantitative Forschung: quantitative research
die Quelle: source
der Querschnitt: cross section
der representative Querschnitt: representative sample
das Quota-Sampling: quota sampling
das Quotenverfahren: quota sampling

das Randomverfahren: random sampling

der Saisonindex: seasonal index
die Schreibtischarbeit: desk work
die Sekundärdaten: secondary material
das Sekundärmaterial: secondary material
die Statistik: statistic
die Steuererleichterung: tax relief
die Stichprobe: random test, sample

die angepasste Stichprobe: balanced sample
die einseitig betonte Stichprobe: biased sample
die representative Stichprobe: representative sample
die Stichprobenanalyse: quota samples
die Stichprobenerhebung: sample survey

das Tiefinterview: depth interview
die Teilmasse: partial statistical 'universe'
der projektive Test: T.A.T. (Thematical Apperceptional Test)
der Trend: trend

die Umfrage: survey
der Umsatz: turnover, sales figure

der Verbraucher: consumer
die Verbraucherforschung: consumer research
die Verbrauchergewohnheit: consumer buying habit
das Verbraucherpanel: consumer panel
die Verkaufsprognose: sales forecast
die Vertriebsforschung: marketing research
das Vertriebsprogramm: marketing plan

die Werbeforschung: advertising research
der Wettbewerb: competition
die Wirtschaftsinformation: economic information

das Zahlenmaterial: data, figures
das Zufallsverfahren: random sampling

Commercial Notes on Export Market Research

1. The purpose (Zweck) of export market research (Auslandsmarktforschung) is to gather information about the:

   country:
   import and export statistics (Ein- und Ausfuhrstatistiken), customs duties (Einfuhrzölle), population (Bevölkerung), etc., etc.

market for the product:
buying power (Kaufkraft) of the population, demand (Nachfrage), activity of the competition (Konkurrenzsituation).

distribution of the product:
distribution channels (Absatzwege), packaging (Verpackung), advertising (Reklame/Werbung), consumer buying habits (Verbrauchergewohnheiten).

reasons for buying the product:
buying motives (Kaufmotive), etc.

This research is either quantitative (quantitative Forschung) i.e. concerned with the facts (Tatsachen) and statistics (Statistiken) or qualitative (qualitativ) i.e. concerned with the reasons (Entscheidungsgründen) and motive (Motiven).

It forms the basis of the sales forecast (Verkaufsprognose) and the marketing plan (Absatzplan).

There are basically two methods by which market research is carried out. The indirect method (indirekte Methode), which is used to gather secondary material (Sekundärdaten) and the direct method (direkte Methode) which is used to gather primary material (Primärdaten).

2. The indirect method

This consists of a study of archive material (Archivmaterial) and published data (publiziertes Zahlenmaterial) and it is known as secondary material. This kind of data consists of regulations (Bestimmungen), indices (Indexzahlen), statistics (Statistiken) and percentage distributions (Prozentanteile). It can be classified as follows:

2.1 *Research about the country*
Import and export statistics (Import/Export Statistiken)
Balance of payments (Aussenhandelsbilanz), etc. For example, in 1971 Federal German imports were as follows:

	Million (DM)
Netherlands	16,603
France	16,298
U.S.A.	14,985
Italy	12,403
Belgium/Luxembourg	11,903
Great Britain	9,641
Switzerland	6,854
Japan	2,220

Import quotas (Einfuhrkontingente)
If there are quota restrictions (Einfuhrkontingente), whether import licences (Einfuhrlizensen) are required. At the moment almost all imports from the U.K. are liberalised (liberalisiert) and no import licences are required.

Exchange control (Devisenkontrolle)
At the moment there are no special requirements regarding exchange control (Devisenkontrolle) as far as Federal Germany is concerned.

Customs duties and taxes (Einfuhrzölle und Steuern)
What customs duties (Einfuhrzölle) apply to the product in question and what rate of V.A.T. (Mehrwertsteuer) is in force. Whether there are any forms of tax relief (Steuererleichterung) for local firms, thereby improving their competitiveness (Konkurrenzfähigkeit).

General economic information (Wirtschaftsinformation)
Population (Bevölkerung), gross national product (Brutto-Sozialprodukt), average income (Durchschnittseinkommen), buying power (Kaufkraft), etc.

2.2 *Research about the market for the product*
Industrial production (Industrielle Produktion)
In 1971, for example, the number of fanheaters produced in West Germany was 950 382. Their value was DM 39 636 000. In 1972 the figures were 923 672 and DM 42 104 000 respectively.

Import and export statistics
For example, in 1971 Germany imported 35,218 fan heaters, of which 3,106 were from the U.K. The figures for 1972 were 17,388 and 1,464 respectively. In 1972 she exported 197,607 fan heaters.

Sales figures (Umsatz)
The sales figures (Umsatz) for the product in the country in question.

Information relating to potential buyers
Number and size (Zahl und Grösse) of households (Haushalte), income (Einkommen), buying power (Kaufkraft), average age (Durchschnittsalter) and occupation (Beruf) of people who have bought the product. Buying habits (Einkaufsgewohnheiten), etc.

2.3 *Sources of information*
Secondary material can be obtained from a variety of sources (Quellen), the following being the main ones:

(a) *Sources in the United Kingdom*
Department of Trade, Statistics and Marketing Intelligence Library, Export House, 50 Ludgate Hill, London, EC4 M7HV. (Tel 01-248-5757). Also: The Export Services and Promotion Division

and the Economics and Statistics Division at the above address, and at regional offices throughout the country.

Confederation of British Industry (C.B.I.), 21 Tothill Street, London SW1. (Tel 01-930-6711). Provides members with fortnightly 'Overseas Trade Bulletin' and with statistical information on request.

London Chamber of Commerce, German Section, 69 Cannon Street, London, EC4. (Tel. 01-248 4444). Contains many reference books and relevant newspaper cuttings.

The Embassy of the Federal Republic of Germany (Die Botschaft der Bundesrepublik Deutschland), 23 Belgrave Square, London, SW1.

Federal German Embassy Commercial Information Office, 6 Rutland Gate, London, SW7. (Tel. 01-584 1271).

German Chamber of Industry and Commerce, 11 Grosvenor Crescent, London, SW1X 7E2. (Tel. 01-235 9947).

Federation of German Industries (B.D.I.), 33 Bruton Street, London, W1. (Tel. 01-499 5852).

Sources in West Germany

Federal Statistics Office (Statistisches Bundesamt), D-62 Wiesbaden, Gustav Stresemann Ring 11. (For all statistics of general importance in Western Germany. Publishes 'Statistisches Jahrbuch für die Bundesrepublik Deutschland'.)

IFo-Institut für Wirtschaftsforschung, D-8 München 27, Poschingerstrasse 5. (For information on general business trends and trends in particular branches of industry.)

Hamburger Welt-Wirtschafts-Archiv, D-2 Hamburg 36, Karl Muck Platz 1. (Keeps extensive archives of German and other commercial publications, etc.)

Institut für Handelsforschung an der Universität Köln, D-5 Köln-Lindenthal. (Makes regular surveys on the structure of and trends in the retail and wholesale trades.)

Deutsche Bundesbank, D-6 Frankfurt/Main, Taunusanlage 4-6. (Publishes a monthly report containing general commercial and specialised financial information—available on request in German and English.)

Association of German Chambers of Commerce (Deutscher Industrie & Handelstag), D-53 Bonn, Adenauer Allee 140. (Members of the Association publish regular bulletins containing information of a general and local nature; there are Chambers of Commerce in most large towns.)

Federation of German Industries (Bundesverband der Deutschen Industrie e.V.), D-5 Köln 10, Habsburgerring 2-12.

H.M. Minister (Economic), British Embassy, D-53 Bonn, Friedrich Ebert Allee 77. (Tel. 22 20 21) and H.M. Consulates in Berlin, Düsseldorf, Frankfurt/Main, Hamburg, Hannover, München and Stuttgart.

British Trade Council in Germany e.V., Secretariat, c/o British Embassy, Bonn. (A voluntary association of British businessmen in Germany which is prepared to assist and advise visiting businessmen from the U.K.)

Trade Directories and Reference Books (*Handelsadressbücher und Nachschlagewerke*)
ABC der Deutschen Wirtschaft, Quellenwerk für Einkauf & Verkauf (Annually), ABC Verlagsgesellschaft G.m.b.H., D-6100 Darmstadt. (Obtainable from Publishing and Distributing Co. Ltd., 177 Regent Street, London W1R 8HR.)

Deutschland Liefert, (Annually), Gemeinschaftsverlag G.m.b.H., D-6100-Darmstadt—Spreestrasse. (Obtainable from Publishing and Distributing Co. Ltd., 177 Regent Street, London W1R 8HR.)

Basic Data on the Economy of the Federal Republic of Germany. U.S. Bureau of International Commerce; can be seen at Statistics and Market-Intelligence Library (London).

Hints to Businessmen. The Federal Republic of Germany and West Berlin. (Obtainable from D.T., Export House, 50 Ludgate Hill, London, EC4 7HU.)

Industrie und Handwerk. Published by W. Kohlhammer G.m.b.H., for the Statistisches Bundesamt, Wiesbaden, D-6500-Main-42, Postfach 120.

3. *The direct method*

This consists in the first instance of a survey of the market (Marktanalyse/Marktuntersuchung) carried out by means of field work (Feldarbeit). Its purpose is to gather primary material (Primärdaten) i.e. material relating primarily to the product. This material relates to the buyers (Käufer), consumers (Verbraucher), the competition (Konkurrenz), advertising (Werbung) and distribution channels (Absatzwege). In addition to pure fact-finding (Tatsachenfeststellung) it may include research into buying motives (Motive).

Surveys are carried out by interviewers (Befrager) using questionnaires (Fragebogen). These are designed to ascertain to what extent the demand (Nachfrage) for the product is already covered (gedeckt), where the greatest demand is to be expected and the reason why certain products are bought.

A sample (Stichprobe) of the 'universe' (Gesamtmasse) is selected for the interviews (Interviews). This sample can be taken at random (Random- or Zufallverfahren), e.g. from address lists (Adresslisten) or by the quota method (Quota-Verfahren). Under the latter system the interviewer is free to choose the people he interviews within the quota.

Later, if the manufacturer wishes to keep up-to-date with changes in demand (Bedarfsschwankungen), with the activity of the competition (Konkurrenz) or with changes in the distribution system (Vertriebssystem) he can arrange for a continuous survey (laufende Marktbeobachtung) to be carried out. This is a dynamic (dynamisch) study, as opposed to the picture (Bild) of the market at a particular moment in time (Zeitpunkt) ascertained by the straightforward market survey.

Methods used to follow buying habits (Kaufgewohnheiten) include the setting-up of consumer panels (Verbraucherpanels). These consist of a sample of about 2000 Households (Haushaltungen) which represent the 'universe'. The daily spending (Ausgaben) of the housewife is determined with the help of household diaries (Haushaltstagebücher) or questionnaires. Stock audits (Lagerbestandsaufnahmen) are carried out in a similar way with retailers (Einzelhändler).

Motivation surveys (Motivforschungen) are designed to ascertain the motives (Motive) and the motivation (Motivierung) of buyers. An explanation is sought, for example, of why a certain brand (eine bestimmte Marke) is being bought.

Techniques include depth interviews (Tiefeninterviews), T.A.T.— i.e. Thematical Apperceptional Tests (Projektive Tests), Recall Tests (Erinnerungsteste) and group discussions (Gruppendiskussionen).

3.1 Conducting market surveys

Although some large international companies carry out field research with their own teams of interviewers, it is more usual to commission one of the market research organisations (Marktforschungsinstitute) or the market research department (Marktforschungsabteilung) of an advertising agency (Werbeagentur). There are a number of market research organisations in the U.K. with subsidiaries or associates in Germany. Their names can be obtained from:

Export Marketing Research Adviser
Export Services Promotion Division
Export House
50 Ludgate Hill, London, EC4 M7HU.   (Tel. 01-248 5757)

There are many such organisations in Germany, some of the major ones being:

Attwood Institut für Marktanalyse G.m.b.H., Wetzlar, Karl Kellner-Ring 23.

DIVO, Institut für Wirtschaftsforschung, Sozialforschung und angewandte Mathematik, Frankfurt/Main, Am Hauptbahnhof 12.

EMNID-Institut (Deutsches Gallup-Institut), Bielefeld, Bodelschwingstr. 23-25a.

GfK, Gesellschaft für Konsum, Markt- und Absatzforschung, Nürnberg, Burgschmietstr. 2.

Infratest—Marktforschung, Motivforschung, Sozialforschung G.m.b.H., München, Schillerstr. 40.

Institut für Demoskopie Allensbach, Gesellschaft zum Studium der öffentlichen Meinung G.m.b.H., Allensbach am Bodensee.

Intermarket, Gesellschaft für internationale Markt- und Meinungsforschung G.m.b.H., Düsseldorf, Kapellstr. 27.

Mafo-Institut, Institut für Markt-, Meinungs- und Absatzforschung G.m.b.H., Frankfurt/Main, Westendplatz 32.

Additional names can be obtained from the Society for Opinion and Marketing Research, (ESOMAR), Raadhuisstraat 15, Amsterdam, or from the British partner of this society, which is the British Market Research Society, 51 Charles Street, London, W1X 7PA.

Letters requesting Information about the Market

1. As you know local conditions so well, we should be most grateful if you would supply us with information about the state of the market in your country.

   Da Sie sicherlich bestens mit den einheimischen Verhältnissen vertraut sind, wären wir Ihnen sehr dankbar wenn Sie uns über die Marktlage in Ihrem Land berichten würden.

2. We would like information on current prices of the following equipment:

   Wir wären Ihnen dankbar für Einzelangaben über den derzeitigen Stand der Preise bei folgenden Geräten:

2. Please let us have details of those products which are in direct competition with our own.

   Bitte senden Sie uns nähere Angaben über diejenigen Produkte die mit den unserigen in direktem Wettbewerb stehen.

Vocabulary

die Abfertigung: clearance, forwarding
die Abgaben (pl.): dues, fees
der Abgangshafen: port of departure
das Abhandenkommen: loss (being mislaid)
der Ablauf (eines Vertrages): expiry of (a contract)
ablehnen: to refuse
der Absatz: sale, marketing, distribution (of goods)
die Absatzfähigkeit: marketability
die Absatzforschung: marketing research
das Absatzgebiet: sales or marketing territory
die Absatzmethode: marketing method
der Absatzplan: marketing plan
die Absatzprognose: marketing forecast
die Absatzstatistik: marketing statistic
der Absatzweg: distribution channel
die Absatzziffer: sales figure
der Absender: consignor, shipper
der Absenderspediteur: forwarding carrier
absetzen: to sell or distribute
abschliessen (Vertrag): to sign a contract
abschliessen (eine Versicherung): to effect an insurance
der Abteilungsleiter: department manager
der Abzahlungskauf: hire purchase
abziehen: to deduct (from payment)
die 'ad hoc' Survey: 'ad hoc' survey
die Adressenkartei: card index or address list
die Adressenliste: address list
der Agent: agent
die Agentur: agency
die Agenturprovision: agency commission
der Agenturvertrag: agency agreement
das Akkdreditiv: letter of credit
die Aktiengesellschaft (A.G.): limited company
akzeptieren: to accept
das Alleinrecht: exclusive right
das Alleinverkaufsrecht: exclusive selling right
der Alleinvertreter: exclusive agent
die Alleinvertretung: exclusive agency
anbieten: to quote
die Änderung: change
den Anforderungen entsprechen: to meet with the requirements
die Anfrage: enquiry
die Angabe(n): particular(s), detail(s)
das Angebot: offer, quotation, supply (as in supply and demand)
das befristete Angebot: offer of limited duration
das freibleibende Angebot: offer subject to alteration
das kombinierte Angebot: combined offer
das preisgünstige Angebot: special offer
das unverbindliche Angebot: offer without obligation (not binding)
die Annahme: assumption
annehmen: to accept (an offer)
der Anreiz: incentive
die Anschlagsäule: advertisement pillar
die Anschlagwerbung: post or outdoor advertising
der Anschluss: connection
ansprechen: to appeal to (as advertisement to customer)
die Anzahlung: deposit
die Anzeige: advertisement
die kleine Anzeige (Kleinanzeige): 'classified' advertisement
die Anzeigenhäufigkeit: frequency of insertion
der Anzeigeninhalt: (advertising) copy
das Anzeigenklischee: advertising block
das Anzeigenmaterial: advertising copy
der Anzeigenpreis: advertising rate
die Anzeigenpreisliste: advertising card
der Anzeigenraum: advertisement space
der Anzeigentext: (advertising) copy
die Anzeigenwerbung: (print or press) advertising
die Archivalien: records/archive material
das Archivmaterial: records/archive material
A.R.D. (Arbeitsgemeinschaft der Rundfunkgesellschaften Deutschlands): 1st T.V. channel (regional commercial)

VOCABULARY—GERMAN/ENGLISH 109

aufheben (einen Vertrag): to cancel (a contract)
der Aufkleber: adhesive label
die Auflage (einer Zeitung u.s.w.): circulation (of a newspaper, etc.)
der Aufschlag: mark-up
aufsetzen (einen Vertrag): to draw up (a contract)
der Aufsteller: display board
der Auftrag (Aufträge): order(s)
einen Auftrag aufgeben: to place an order
einen Auftrag erteilen: to place an order
der Auftragseingang: receipt of an order
die Auftragserledigung: execution of an order
das Auftragsformular: order form
der Auftraggeber: consignor, principal (e.g. of agent or of client for whom a research company works)
der Auftragnehmer: agent (in legal sense)
die Ausbildung: training
ausdrücklich: expressly
die Ausfertigung: copy (of B/L., etc.)
die Ausfuhr: export
die Ausfuhrbewilligung: export licence
die Ausfuhrstatistiken: export statistics
die Ausführung: the design, construction, execution
aushändigen: to hand over (B/L., etc.)
um Auskunft bitten: to ask for information
das Auslagefenster: show window
die Auslandsmarktforschung: export market research
der Auslandsvertreter: overseas agent
auspacken: to unpack
der Aussenstand: outstanding debt
verlorene Aussenstände: bad debts
ausstellen: to display
der Ausstellkasten: showcase
die Ausstellungsfläche: display area
der Ausstellungsraum: showroom
die Auswertung: evaluation

mit der Bahn schicken: to send by rail
der (Bahn) Frachtbrief: (rail) consignment note
der Ballen: bale
der Bankrott: bankruptcy (ordinary)

der fahrlässige Bankrott: bankruptcy (reckless)
Bankrott machen: to go or to become bankrupt
die Bankspesen: bank charges
die (Bank) Überweisung: (bank) transfer
das Bargeschäft: cash transaction
barzahlen: to pay cash
die Barzahlung: cash payment
der Bedarf: requirements
beenden (ein Vertragsverhältnis): to terminate (a contract)
befördern: to transport or to ship
die Beförderung: carriage, forwarding
direkte Beförderung: direct dispatch
die Beförderungsart: method of transport
der Beförderungsvertrag: contract of carriage
der Befrager: interviewer
der Befragte: interviewee
die Befragung: interview
beglaubigen: to certify
die Beglaubigung: certification
begleichen: to pay (a debt)
die Begutachtung: expert opinion
der Behälter: container
der Behälterverkehr: container traffic
behandeln: to handle
der Behälterumschlagplatz: container depot
beifügen: to enclose (with letter, etc.)
beladen: to load
benennen (p.p. benannt): to specify, to name
benötigen: to need
die Beratung: advice
berechnen: to calculate
berichtigen: to rectify, to correct
die Beschädigung: damage
die Beschaffenheit: nature (of goods)
beschreiben: to describe
bestätigen: to confirm
bestätigt: confirmed (as L/C.)
die Bestätigung: confirmation/acknowledgement
bestellen: to order
die Bestellung: order
der Bestellschein: order form
der Bestellzettel: order form

bestimmen: to define
der Betrag: amount
der Betriebsführer: managing director or works manager
der Betriebsleiter: works manager
die Betriebsunkosten: overheads
die Bevölkerung: population
der Beweis: proof
beweisen: to prove, demonstrate
die Bezeichnung(-en): description(s)
der Bezirksvertreter: area agent
das Billigkeitsrecht: law of equity
sich binden: to bind oneself (by contract)
der Binnentarif: intra E.E.C. tariff
der Binnentransport: inland transport
der Blickfang: eye-catcher/advertising stunt
der Bogen: sheet (of paper)
die Bonität: solvency, good standing
brauchen: to require, to need
brechen (einen Vertrag): to break a contract
die Broschüre: brochure
Brüsseler Zolltarif Schema: Brussels nomenclature
das Bruttosozialprodukt: gross national product
die Bundesbahn: German State Railway
bürgen: to vouch for, to guarantee
der Bürobedarf: office supplies
die Bürounkosten: office expenses

der Chartervertrag: the charter party
(der) Cash-and-Carry Betrieb (C. & C. Betrieb): cash and carry
der Chef der Einkaufsabteilung: head buyer
der Container: container
offener Container: open-top container
Container mit Seitentüren: container with side doors
die Container-Abfertigungsanlage: container (dispatch) depot (with customs office)
die Container-Anlage: container depot
das Container-Depot: container depot
der Containerdienst: container service
der Container-Lagerplatz: container depot

der Container-Sammelgutverkehr: container groupage traffic
der Container-Schnellzug: container express train
das Container-Spezialfahrzeug: special container vehicle
das Container-Terminal: container terminal
der Container-Transport: container transport
der Container-Umschlagplatz: container (transfer) depot
der Coupon: coupon

die Dauerhaftigkeit: durability
der Debitsaldo: balance payable
der Deckel: lid, cover
die Delkredereprovision: 'del credere' commission
Deutsche Bundesbahn: German State Railway
die Devisenkontrolle: exchange control
das Diapositiv: transparency
die Dienstleistung: service
die Dienstleistungskosten: service costs
der Dienstvertrag: service agreement
D.I.N. (Deutsches Institut für Normen): German Standards Institute (equivalent to B.S.I.)
die direkte Methode: direct method
der Direktor: director
die Direktwerbung: direct mail-advertising
das Diskonthaus: discount house
diskontieren: to discount
das Display-Material: display material
die Dockanlage: dock
der Dockarbeiter: docker
das Dokumentenakkreditiv: documentary letter of credit
die Dokumententratte: documentary draft
Dokumente gegen Wechselakzept: documents against acceptance (D/A)
Dokumente gegen Zahlung: documents against payment (D/P)
Drittes (III.) Programm: Third T.V. channel (regional, non-commercial)
der Dritte: third party
die Durchfahrt: transit

die Durchfuhr: transit
der Durchgangstarif: through rate
der Durchgangswagen: through railway-wagon
durchgehender Container-Transport: through-container-transport
das Durchkonnossement: 'through' bill of lading
der Durchschnitt: average
die Durchschnittsbestimmung: average-analysis
die Durchschnittserhebung: average-analysis
das Düsenflugzeug: jet plane

die Eigenart: characteristic
der Eigenhändler: businessman (trading on his own account)
das Eigentumsrecht: (right of) ownership
der Eigentumsvorbehalt: reservation of proprietary rights
die Eigentumsübertragung: transfer of ownership
das Eilgut: express goods
der Eilgüterzug: fast goods train
einbehalten: to deduct (from payment)
die Einfuhr: import
die Einfuhrbewilligung: import licence
die Einfuhrgenehmigung: import licence
das Einfuhrkontingent: import quota
die Einfuhrlizenz: import licence
die Einfuhrstatistiken: import statistics
der Einfuhrzoll: import duty
einhalten: to keep to (delivery date)
einhalten (eine Vertragsbestimmung): to conform or keep to a clause in a contract
die Einheitsladung: unit load
der zentrale Einkauf: central buying
die Einkaufsabteilung: buying department
der Einkaufschef: head buyer
die Einkaufsgenossenschaft: co-operative buying association
die Einkaufsgewohnheit: buying habit
die zentrale Einkaufsorganisation: central buying organisation
der Einkaufspreis: purchase price
der Einkaufsverband: purchasing group

die Einkaufszentrale: central buying organisation
das Einkommen: income
die Einleitung: introduction
einlösen: to cash in (a coupon, etc.)
einpacken: to pack
die Einschränkung: restriction or reservation
das Einschreibepäckchen: registered packet
das Einschreibepaket: registered parcel
einsetzen: to appoint
der Einstandspreis: cost price
eintreffen (in): to arrive (at a destination)
die Einwegkiste: non-returnable box
der Einzelhändler: retailer
das Einzelhandelsgeschäft: retail shop
der Einzelhandelspreis: retail price
die Einzelpolice: single policy
die Einziehung von Schulden: debt collecting
die Eisenbahnbeförderung: railway transport
das Eisenbahn-Container Schiff: container rail-ferry
der Eisenbahnfähre-Sammelwaggon: rail-ferry container wagon
der Empfang: reception
der Empfänger: recipient, consignee
die Empfangsbestätigung: acknowledgement of receipt
der Endlader: container with doors at rear or both ends
die Enquete: survey, enquiry, poll
das Entgelt: remuneration
entladen: to unload
entlassen: to dismiss
die Entlohnung: remuneration
entschädigen: to indemnify
sich entscheiden: to decide
der Entwurf: design
der Erfüllungsort: place of delivery
erheben: to collect, levy (tax, etc.)
die Erhebung: survey
der Erinnerungstest: recall test
erlauben: to allow, permit
erledigen: to settle (business)
erleiden (Schaden): to suffer (damage or loss)
ernennen: to appoint

erneuern: to renew (a contract)
die Erneuerung: renewal
eröffnen (ein Geschäft): to open a shop/business
eröffnen: to open (an account, a letter of credit)
erteilen (einen Auftrag): to place an order
erwerben (Versicherungspolice): to take out (insurance policy)
Europäische Wirtschaftsgemeinschaft (E.W.G.): European Economic Community (E.E.C.)
eventuell: possible
die Expansion: expansion
die Exportabteilung: export department
der Exportleiter: exporter manager
die Exportkiste: export packing case
die Exportverpackung: export packing
das Expressgut: express parcel service

der Fabrikleiter: works manager
das Fachblatt/die Fachzeitschrift: specialist periodical, trade journal
das Fachgeschäft: specialist shop
der Fachkaufmann: specialist
der Fährboot-Waggon: train ferry wagon
die Fähre: ferry (-boat)
die Fahrlässigkeit: negligence
grobe Fahrlässigkeit: gross negligence
das Fährschiff: ferry or train ferry
das Fahrzeug: vehicle
das begleitete Fahrzeug: driver-accompanied vehicle
fällig: due
fällig werden: to become due, to mature (a bill)
die Fälligkeit: maturity (of bill)
bei Fälligkeit: at maturity
fehlerhaft: faulty, defective, deficient
die Feldarbeit: field work
der farbige Fernsehspot: colour-T.V. advertisement or spot
die Fernsehwerbung: T.V. advertising
der Fernspediteur: long-distance haulier
die Fertigungsgemeinkosten: factory overheads
das Festangebot: firm offer
die Fibertrommel: fibre-drum (for packing)

(als) Fideikommiss besitzen: to hold in trust
die Filiale: branch (legally dependent on parent company)
der Filialbetrieb: branch (legally dependent on parent company)
finanziell: financial
imaterieller Firmenwert: goodwill of a business
die Fixkosten: fixed expenses
der FLEI-Verkehr (Flugzeug/Eisenbahnverkehr): air/rail traffic
das Flugblatt: handbill/leaflet
die Fluglinie: airline
die Flugverkehrsgesellschaft: airline
das Flugzeug: aeroplane
das Formular: the form
die Forschung: research
die qualitative Forschung: qualitative research
die quantitative Forschung: quantitative research
die Fracht: cargo, freight
der Frachtbrief: consignment note, way bill
frachtfrei: carriage paid (C.P. or CGE. paid)
der Frachtführer: freight carrier
Fracht gegen Nachnahme: freight forward
das Frachtgut: freight or cargo
die Frachtkosten: freight charges
Frachtkosten per Nachnahme: carriage forward
allgemeine Frachtraten: general cargo rates
das Frachtschiff: cargo boat
der Frachtvertrag: contract of carriage
der Fragebogen: questionnaire
frei an Bord/franko Bord: free on board (F.O.B.)
frei Bahnwagen: free on rail (F.O.R.)
frei Güterwagen/Lastkraftwagen: free on truck (F.O.T.)
frei Haus: franco (FCO) domicile
frei Längsseite Schiff: free alongside ship (F.A.S.)
frei Schiff: free on board (F.O.B.)
Frei von Beschädigung ausser im Strandungsfall: F.P.A. policy (free of particular average)

Frei von Beschädigung wenn unter 3%: W.P.A. policy (with particular average)
frei Waggon: free on rail (F.O.R.)
die Frist: time limit, date, deadline
der Fristablauf: deadline, expiration of a period
die Frist einhalten: to meet the deadline
fristlos: without notice
die Full-Service Werbeagentur: full-service advertising agency
der Funkspot: radio commercial
der Funktext: radio script

der Gabelstapler: forklift truck
die Garantie: guarantee
garantieren: to guarantee
der Garantievertreter: 'del credere' agent
das Gebrauchsmuster: sample, registered design
der Gebietsleiter: area manager
die Gebühr: fee, tax, charge, etc.
gedeckt sein: to be held covered
die Gegenleistung: return service
als Gegenleistung: in return for
das Gehalt: salary or wage
festes Gehalt: fixed salary
der Geldbetrag: cash
das Gemischwarengeschäft: general store
der General Cargo Box Container: general cargo box container
die Generalpolice: 'open' policy
der Generalvertreter: general agent
geprüft: checked
das Gericht: court
gerichtlich gegen jemanden vorgehen: to take someone to court
der Gerichtsstand: jurisdiction
die Gesamtmasse: 'universe', population
die Gesamtsumme: total amount
der Gesamtwert: total value
der Geschäftsführer: managing director
das Geschäftsgeheimnis: business or trade secret
das Geschäftsjahr: trading year
ins Geschäft kommen: to do business with
die Geschäftsunkosten: overheads or business expenses

die (Geschäfts) Vertragsfähigkeit: capacity to contract
der Geschenkartikel: gift
die Geschmacksrichtung: taste (in fashion, etc.)
Gesellschaft mit beschränkter Haftung (G.m.b.H./GMBH.): limited company
die Gesellschaftszeitschrift: society magazine
die Gesetzgebung: legislation
gesetzlich: legal
gesetzlich geschützt: protected by law, patented
die Gestaltung: display, presentation, creative work, arrangement, design
die Gestaltungsgruppe: creative division
die Gestaltungskosten: technical costs
die Gestehungskosten: production costs
das Gestell: rack
gesteuert: duty paid
die Gewährleistung: warranty, guarantee
die höhere Gewalt: 'force majeure'
das Gewicht (netto, brutto): weight (net, gross)
der Gewichtszoll: specific duty (based on weight)
der Gewinn: the profit
die Gewinnspanne: profit margin
der Goodwill: goodwill of a business
die Grosseinkaufsgenossenschaft (G.E.G.): bulk-buying co-operative
der Grosshändler: wholesaler
die Grundlage: basis
der Grundpreis: basic price
die Gruppendiskussion: group discussion
gültig: valid
die Gültigkeitsdauer: period of validity
zu Gunsten: in favour of
günstig (Angebot): advantageous (offer)
eine günstige Gelegenheit benutzen: to take advantage of an opportunity
der Güterfernverkehr: long distance road haulage
der Güterzug: goods train
der Guthabensaldo: credit balance
der Gutschein: coupon or voucher

die Hafenanlagen: docks
einen Hafen anlaufen: to call at a port
die Hafengebühren: port dues

haften: to be held liable
die Haftung: liability
handhaben: to handle
der Handler: tradesman, trader, dealer
handeln: to trade
das Handelsadressbuch: trade directory
der Handelsmakler: broker
die Handelsrechnung: commercial invoice
das Handelsrecht: commercial law
die Handelsspanne: (gross) margin
der Handelsvertreter: commercial agent, manufacturer's agent
der Haushalt: household
die Haushaltung: household
das Haushaltstagebuch: housekeeping diary
der Haus-Haus Transport: door-to-door transport
die Hausmarke: own brand
die Havarie: average, damage (by sea)
die grosse (gemeinschaftliche) Havarie: G.A. (general average)
die kleine Havarie: particular average
die Hecktür: rear door
die Holzfaserkiste: wood-fibre box
der Holzverschlag: wooden crate

das Image: image
der Importeur: importer
importieren: to import
die Importlizenz: import licence
die Indexzahl: index figure
indossieren: to endorse
die Informationsquelle: source of information
die Inkassovollmacht: authority to collect (bills of exchange, etc.)
der Inlandsmarkt: home market
der Inlandspreis: home market price
die aktuelle Illustrierte: topical illustrated magazine
das Inserat: advertisement
die Insertionsgebühr: advertising charge
sich für etwas interessieren: to be interested in something
das Interview: interview
die Inverzugsetzung: warning, unconditional request for performance

die Inzahlungnahme: trade-in
die Ist-Zahl: actual figure

der Kai: quay
der Kai-Empfangsschein: mate's receipt
die Kai-Umschlaggebühr: dockside transfer charge
der Karton: carton, cardboard box
die Kartonage: cardboard containers
Kasse gegen Dokumente: cash against documents (C.A.D.)
der Katalog: catalogue
der Käufer: buyer, customer
die Käuferforschung: customer research
die Kaufkraft: buying power
das Kaufmotiv: buying motive
die freiwillige Kette: voluntary chain (of shops)
der Kettenladen: chain store
das Kettenladenunternehmen: chain store business
die Kennziffer: box or code numbers (for adverts)
das Kino: cinema
die Kiste: box
die hölzerne Kiste: wooden box
die Klausel: clause
der Klimaschutz: tropical protection
der Klischeefuss: printing block
der (Kraftfahrzeug)anhänger: lorry trailer
der Kramladen: junk shop
die Kreditfähigkeit: credit worthiness
das Kredithaus: credit house
der Kommissionär: commission agent
die Konjunktur: market conditions, state of the economy
der Konkurrent: competitor
die Konkurrenz: competition
konkurrenzfähig: competitive
konkurrieren: to compete
das Konkursverfahren (normale): (ordinary) bankruptcy
Konkurs machen: to go into bankruptcy, to go bankrupt
das Konossement (rein): (clean) bill of lading
das Konsignationslager: consignment stock

VOCABULARY—GERMAN/ENGLISH

in Konsignation nehmen (Waren): to take (goods) on consignment, to consign
konsignieren: to consign (goods)
die Konsulatfaktura: consular invoice
die Konsumforschung: consumer research
die Konsumgenossenschaft: co-operative society
der Konsumverein: co-operative society
die Kontaktgruppe: 'account group' (for advertising agency)
der Kontaktor: account executive
das Kontingent: quota
der Kontoauszug: statement
auf ein Konto einzahlen: to pay into an account
der Korrosionsschutz: corrosion protection
die Kosten (plur.): costs
der Kostenaufwand: expenditure
der Kostendruck: pressure of costs
Kosten und Fracht: C. & F. (cost and freight)
Kosten, Versicherung, Fracht: cost, insurance, freight (C.I.F.)
variable Kosten: variable costs
das Kubikmass: cubic measure
der Kühl-Container: refrigerated container
der Kunde: customer, client
der Kunde (voraussichtlich, möglich): customer or client (potential)
der Kundendienst: after-sales service
der Kundenkreis: clientele, customers
die Kündigung: dismissal
die Kündigungsfrist: period of notice
die Kundschaft: customers
die Kundschaft übernehmen: to acquire the goodwill of a business
der Kunststoff: plastic
die Kunststoff-Folie: plastic foil
der Kunststoff-Lack: synthetic varnish
der Kursstand: rate of exchange

die Ladeeinheit: unit load
laden: to load
der Laden: shop
die Ladentischauslage: counter display
der Laderaum: cargo hold
das Ladeverzeichnis: manifest
die (volle) Ladung: full load
die Lage: situation, position, standing, status
die finanzielle Lage: financial standing
das Lager: store
ab Lager: ex-warehouse
die Lagerbestandsaufnahme: stock audit
die Lagergebühren: storage charges or costs
die Lagerung: storage
auf Lager halten: to keep in store
die Lagerhaltung: storage
der Lagerumsatz: stock turnover
LASH-Frachter (Schuten auf Seeschiff): LASH, lighter aboard ship
die Last: load
der Lastkraftwagen (LKW): lorry
der Lastzug: trailer-tractor unit
die Lattenkiste: crate
die Lebensdauer: life, service life
der Leiter der Einkaufsabteilung: head buyer
die Leserschaft: readership
der Lesezirkel: reading-circle, magazine library
liberalisieren: to liberalise
der Lieferant: supplier
die Lieferbedingungen: terms of delivery
die Lieferfrist: delivery period
liefern: to supply
der Lieferschein: delivery note
der Liefertermin: delivery date
die Lieferung: supply, delivery
bei Lieferung zahlen: cash on delivery (C.O.D.)
die Lieferzeit: time of delivery
von einer Liste streichen: to take off a list
die Litfasssäule: poster column
die Lohnkosten: labour costs
löschen: to unload a ship
der Luft-Expressdienst: air express service
die Luft-Expressfracht: express airfreight
die Luftfracht: airfreight
der Luftfrachtbrief: air waybill
die Luftfrachtgesellschaft: air-cargo carrier
das Luftfrachtkontor: airway service office

der Luftfrachtspediteur: airway forwarding agent
die Luftpaketpost: air parcel post
die Luftverkehrsgesellschaft: airline
auf dem Luftweg: by air

das Magazin: magazine
der Mal-Nachlass: quantity rebate
der Manager: manager
der Mangel: defect
die Markentreue: brand loyalty
die Markenwerbung: brand advertising
das Marketing: marketing
die Markierung: marking (on a package, etc.)
der Markt: market
heimischer Markt: home market
die Marktanalyse: market survey, market analysis
die Marktbeobachtung: continuous survey
der Marktforscher: market researcher
die Marktforschung: market research
die Marktforschungsgruppe: market research
die Marktuntersuchung: market survey
die charakteristische Markuntersuchung: controlled sample
die regionale Marktuntersuchung: area sample
das Mass: measure
die Massengüter: bulk goods
die Massen-Medien: mass media
massgebend: authoritative
das Material: material
die Materialkosten: material costs
die Mediaforschung: media research
das Medium (pl. Medien, Media): advertising medium
der Mehrfarbendruck: colour print
die Mehrwertsteuer (M.W.St.): value added tax (V.A.T.)
die Menge: quantity, amount
der Mengeneinkauf: bulk purchase
der Mengennachlass: quantity rebate or reduction
der Mengenrabatt: quantity discount
der Mengenzoll: specific duty (based on quantity)
das Merchandising: merchandising

die direkte Methode: direct method
die indirekte Methode: indirect method
die unsaubere Methode: unethical method
die Millimeterhöhe: millimeter height (of an advertisement) (c.f. column-inch)
das Mindesteinkommen: minimum income
der Mitarbeiterstab: team of colleagues
der Mittelwert: average, mean, median
der Monatsabschluss: monthly settlement
die Monatsberechnung: monthly account
motorisiert: motorised, tractor-drawn
die Motivforschung: motivational research
das Muster: sample

die Nachfrage: demand (for goods)
die Nachfristsetzung: extension of time (granted to debtor, etc.)
nachkommen: to meet, comply with
der Nachlass (pl. N'lässe): rebate, discount
gegen Nachnahme: C.O.D., freight forward
unter Nachnahme: C.O.D.
das Nachschlagebuch: reference book
der Nachteil: disadvantage
nachteilig: detrimental or prejudicial
nachweisen (einen Vorteil): demonstrate, to prove (an advantage)
der Normalpreis: regular price
die Normbezeichnung: standard specification
der Nutzen: profit, gain

'oben': 'this side up'
offenlegen: to disclose
die Öffentlichkeitsarbeit: public relations work
die Offerte: offer

das Paket: parcel
als Paket schicken: to send by parcel post
die Palette: pallet
der Pappkarton: cardboard box

die Pappkiste: cardboard case
das Pappmännchen: cardboard figure
die Pappschachtel: cardboard box
passen (jemandem): to fit, to suit (someone)
das Patentrecht: patent right
ein Patent verletzen: to infringe a patent
die Patentverletzung: infringement of a patent
die Pauschalfracht: lump-sum freight
das Pauschalhonorar: fee or payment
die Pauschalpolice: 'flat rate' policy
die Pauschalzahlung: lump sum payment
der Personaldirektor: personnel manager
die Personalkosten: salaries, wages
das Plakat: poster
der Plan: drawing
der Platz: position (of an advertisement on page)
der Platzvertreter: local agent
die Plombe: seal (usually of lead)
plombiert: sealed
die Police: policy
die laufende Police: 'declaration', 'open, or 'floating' policy
der Portier: gatekeeper
die Position: item
die Post: postal service, post office
der Posten: item
die Postgebühren: postal charges
der Postscheck: postal cheque
die Postversandwerbung: direct mail advertising
die Prämie: bonus, premium
präsentieren: to present (a bill, etc.)
der Preis: price
der äusserste Preis: lowest price, best possible price
der feste Preis: firm price
der konkurrenzfähige Preis: competitive price
der niedrigste Preis: lowest price
ein mässiger Preis: a reasonable price
einen Preis berechnen, kalkulieren: to arrive at a price, to calculate a price
einen Preis erhöhen, heraufsetzen, steigern: to raise a price
einen Preis ermässigen, herabsetzen, senken: to reduce, lower a price

der Preisaufschlag: increase in price, extra charge
das Preisausschreiben: competition (with prizes)
Preise angeben: to quote prices
ein Preisangebot machen: to submit an offer/a quotation
die Preiserhöhung: price increase
die Preisermässigung: price reduction
die Preislage: price range
die Preisliste: price list
der Preisnachlass: price reduction
die Preisschwankung: fluctuation in price
die Preisskala: price range
die Preisüberwachung: price control
die Preisverordnung: price regulation
das Preisverzeichnis: price list
die Prestigewerbung: prestige advertising
die Primärdaten: primary material
das Primärmaterial: primary material
die Probe: sample
der Probeabzug: proof (sheet), pull
die Probezeit: trial period
die Produktforschung: product research
die Produktionsgruppe: production division
der Produktionsleiter: production manager
der Profit: profit
die Proformarechnung: proforma invoice
die Programmzeitschrift: programme magazine
der Prokurist: manager or head clerk (with power to sign binding contracts and to represent the firm in a court of law)
die Promptzahlung: prompt payment
der Prospekt: prospectus
das Prospektmaterial: advertising copy
die Provision: commission
der Provisionsvertreter: commission agent
der Provisionssatz: rate of commission
der Prozentanteil: percentage
die Public-Relations-Gruppe: public relations division
prüfen: to check

das Prüfen: checking
zur Prüfung: on trial

die Qualität: quality
die qualitative Forschung: qualitative research
die Quantität: quantity
die quantitative Forschung: quantitative research
das Quartal: quarter (three months)
die Quartalsabrechnung: quarterly statement of account
die Quartalsrechnung: quarterly bill
die Quartalszahlung: quarterly payment
die Quelle: source
der Querschnitt: cross section
der repräsentative Querschnitt: representative sample
quittieren (eine Rechnung): to receipt an invoice
die Quittung: receipt
die Quote: quota
das Quotenverfahren: quota sampling
das Quota-Sampling: quota sampling

der Rabatt (pl. Rabatte): rebate, discount
das Randomverfahren: random sampling
die Rate: instalment
die Ratenzahlung: payment by instalments
der Raum: room or space
der Rauminhalt: capacity, volume
die Raumkosten: cost of premises
die Rechnung: bill, account
auf eigene Rechnung handeln: to conduct business on one's own account
laufende Rechnung: open account
in laufender Rechnung stehen: to have an open account
offene Rechnung: open account
der vierteljährliche Rechnungsabschluss: quarterly credit
der Rechnungsbetrag: total amount
das Rechnungsjahr: financial year
das Recht: law or right
das massgebende Recht: applicable law
rechtskräftig sein: to have the force of law

die Reederei: shipper (shipping company)
die Reichweite: coverage
der Reinverdienst: nett profit
die Reinzeichnung: final art work
das Reisegeld: travelling allowance
die Reisekosten: travelling expenses
die Reisespesen: travelling expenses
die Reklame: advertising, advertisement, publicity
der Restbetrag: balance
der Richtpreis: standard price, price recommended by manufacturer but which trade is not obliged to adopt
das Risiko: risk
der Rohgewinnaufschlag: mark-up
die Rohskizze: layout
eine bedeutende Rolle spielen: to play an important part
das Rollgeld: cartage
die Rollspesen: cartage
der Ro-Ro Frachter: roll-on/roll-off ferry ship
der Rundfunk: radio

der Saisonindex: seasonal index
der Saldo: balance
der Sammeleinkauf: group buying
der Sammelgutschein: voucher (for collecting)
der Sammelgutverkehr: groupage traffic
die Sammelladung: groupage consignment
die Sammellieferung: bulk delivery
der Sammeltransport: collective or groupage transport
der Schaden: damage
der Schadenersatz: compensation, damages
Schadenersatzklage erheben: to sue for damages
schadenersatzpflichtig: liable to pay damages
das Schaufenster: shop window
der Scheck: cheque
schicken: to send
das Schiedsgericht: court of arbitration
der Schiedsrichter: arbitrator
der Schiedsspruch: arbitration

Schiedsspruch erledigen: by arbitration
das Schiedsverfahren: arbitration
die Schiffahrtsgesellschaft: shipping company
die Schiffsladung: cargo
'in Schiffswahl': a shipowner has the right to decide whether the goods are to be charged by volume or weight
der Schiffszusammenstoss: collision at sea
das Schlagwort: slogan
die Schleichwerbung: covert advertising (editorials, etc.)
die Schlichtung: conciliation
die Schreibtischarbeit: desk work
schriftlich bestätigen: to confirm in writing
der Schriftsatz: composition, type
die Schulung: training
der Schuppen: shed
die Stahlbandverschnürung: steel bands (for securing a case)
der Stammkunde: longstanding customer
das Standardformat: standard size
der standard Stahl-Container: standard steel container
der Ständer: stand (in shop)
der (Messe) Stand: (exhibition) stand
die Statistik: statistic
die Stellung: position, job
die Stereotypieplatte: 'stereo' or block
die Steuererleichterung: tax relief
die Stichprobe: random test, sample
die angepasste Stichprobe: balanced sample
die einseitig betonte Stichprobe: biased sample
die repräsentative Stichprobe: representative sample
die Stichprobenanalyse: quota sample
die Stichprobenerhebung: sample survey
der Stoss (pl. Stösse): knock or impact(s)
die Stossfestigkeit: impact resistance
die Stosskraft: impact (of an advertisement)
stören: to disturb
die Strafklausel: penalty clause
die Strandung: stranding, shipwreck
im Strandungsfall: in case of shipwreck
der Strassengüterverkehr: road haulage

streichen (von einer Liste): to withdraw (from a list)
der Streik: strike
der wilde Streik: wildcat strike
der Streit: the dispute
einen Streit durch Schiedsspruch erledigen: to settle a dispute by arbitration
die Streitsache: case under dispute
die Streubreite: coverage
streuen: to distribute
die Streukosten: media expenditure, space charge, coverage costs
der Streuplan: space schedule
die Streuplanung: media strategy
die Streuung: media planning, media schedule, coverage
die Streuungsgruppe: media planning division
der Streuweg: media chosen for campaign
die Stückzahl: quantity
der Stückzoll: specific duty
das Stückgut: piece goods
der Schutz: protection
schützen: to protect
die Schutzvorrichtung: safeguard
die Schwingungen: vibrations
die Schweizer Bundesbahn (S.B.B.): Swiss State Railway
die Seefrachtrate: seafreight rate
seefrachtmässig: seaworthy
seetüchtig: seaworthy
die Seite: page
der Seitenpreis: page rate
der Seitenteil: part page
die Sekundärdaten: secondary material
das Sekundärmaterial: secondary material
der Selbstkostenpreis: cost of production, net cost
der Selbstbedienungsladen (S.B.-Laden): self-service shop
das Selbstbedienungswarenhaus: self-service store
selbständig: independent
durchgehend palettisierter Service: through pallet service
sittenwidrig: unethical
die Sichttratte: sight or demand draft or bill

der **Sichtwechsel**: sight or demand draft (D.D.)
der **Sitz (einer Vertretung)**: head office (of an agency)
die **Skizze**: sketch
die **Soll-Vorgabe**: budgeted target
die **Sollzahl**: forecast figure
das **Sonderangebot**: special offer
die **Sondervorschrift**: special rule or regulation
die **Sonntagszeitung**: Sunday paper
das **Sortiment**: assortment or collection or range of goods
das **Sortimentgeschäft**: general store
die **Spaltenzahl**: number of columns
der **Spediteur**: carrier or forwarding agent
die **Spediteurübernahmebescheinigung**: certificate of shipment
die **internationale Spedition**: international forwarding
der **Speditionsvertrag**: contract of carriage
das **Sperrgut**: bulky goods
die **Sperrholzkiste**: plywood case
die **Spesen**: expenses
das **Spezialgeschäft**: specialist shop
suchen: to look for
der **Supermarkt**: supermarket

30 **Tage netto**: 30 days net
die **Tageszeitung**: daily paper
die **Tara (Gewicht)**: tare (weight)
die **Tarifeinordnung**: tariff classification
die **Taxe**: valuation, assessment
das **Teerpapier**: tarred paper
der **Teilbetrag**: instalment
die **Teilmasse**: partial statistical 'universe'
die **Teilseite**: part-page
die **Teilzahlung**: instalment
die **Teilzahlungsrate**: instalment
die **Telefonzelle**: telephone box
die **Telefonzentrale**: telephone exchange
die **Tendenz**: tendency
der **Termin**: deadline
der **projektive Test**: T.A.T. (Thematical Apperceptional Test)
der **Testmarkt**: test market
das **Tiefinterview**: depth interview

die **Tochtergesellschaft**: subsidiary company (legally independent)
die **Tragfähigkeit**: carrying capacity
der **Trailer**: trailer
der **Traktor**: tractor
das **Transportdokument**: shipping document
die **Transportkosten**: transport costs or carriage
das **Transportunternehmen**: haulage firm
der **Transportunternehmer**: haulier
die **Tratte**: draft
der **Trend**: trend
treuhänderisch verwalten: to hold in trust
die **Trödelbude**: junk shop or old clothes shop
die **T.V.-Werbung**: T.V. advertising

die **Übergangszeit**: transition period
überlegen: to think over
übernehmen (eine Vertretung): to take on (an agency)
überschreiten: to exceed
die **Überseezeit**: ferry time
übertragbar: negotiable, transferable
übertragen: to transfer, to transmit
sich überzeugen: to convince oneself
die **Umfrage**: survey
umladen: to transfer, to reload
umrechnen: to convert (money)
der **Umsatz**: turnover or 'billing'
unbestätigt: unconfirmed
unbestimmt: indefinite
die **allgemeinen Unkosten**: general overheads
die **Unterlage**: documentation, 'literature'
der **Unternehmer**: principal
der **Unternehmergewinn**: employer's profit
der **Untervertreter**: sub-agent
unverbindlich: not binding
unverzollt: duty unpaid
unwiderruflich: irrevocable
das **Ursprungszeugnis**: certificate of origin

der **Verbraucher**: consumer
die **Verbraucherforschung**: consumer research

die Verbrauchergewohnheit: consumer buying habit
der Verbrauchermarkt: retail cash and carry store
das Verbraucherpanel: consumer panel
verbreiten: distribute, circulate (catalogues)
das Verbreitungsgebiet: distribution area
das Verbrennen: burning
der Verderb: destruction
vereinbaren (einen Preis): to agree (a price)
der Verkäufer: salesman
der technische Verkäufer: technical sales representative
die (Verkaufs)filiale: branch (legally dependent on parent company)
die Verkaufsfläche: sales area
die Verkaufsförderung: sales promotion
die Verkaufsgewandtheit: skill in selling
der Verkaufsingenieur: sales engineer
der Verkaufsleiter: sales manager
die Verkaufsleitung: sales management
das Verkaufspersonal: sales personnel
der Verkaufsplan: sales budget
die Verkaufsprognose: sales forecast
der Verkaufsschlager: good selling line
das Verkaufsteam: sales team
der Verkaufsvertrag: sales contract
die Verkaufsvoraussage: sales forecast
die Verkaufsunterstützung: merchandising
verladen: to load
die Verladung: loading
verlangen: to demand
der Verlust: loss
die Vernagelung: nailing
verpacken: to pack
die Verpackung: packing or wrapping
Verpackung besonders berechnet: packing charged extra
die innere Verpackung: inner packing
Verpackung zum Wegwerfen: non-returnable packing
die Verpackungsart: method of packing
sich verpflichten: to bind oneself
verrufen: decry
die Versandanzeige: dispatch note
die Versandart: method of dispatch

die Versandanweisungen: forwarding instructions
die Versandanzeige: dispatch note
die Versandbescheinigung: certificate of shipment
das Versandgeschäft: mail order business
das Versandhaus: mail order business
die Versandpapiere: shipping documents
die Versandspesen: forwarding charges
die Versandvorschriften: forwarding instructions
die Verschiffung: shipment, shipping
der Verschiffungshafen: port of embarkation
die Verschollenheit: disappearance
das Versenken: sinking
der Versicherer: insurer/underwriter
der Versicherte: insured
die Versicherung: insurance
die 'all risks' Versicherung: 'all risks' insurance
die Versicherung mit Havarie: W.P.A. Policy
die Versicherung ohne Particular Havarie: F.P.A. policy
der Versicherungsagent: insurance agent
die Versicherungsdeckungsnote: insurance cover note
die Versicherungsgesellschaft: insurance company
der Versicherungsmakler: insurance broker
die Versicherungspolice: insurance policy
das Versicherungszertifikat: insurance certificate
die Verspätung: delay
verteilen: to distribute
der Verteiler: distributor
der Vertrag: contract
einen Vertrag aufsetzen: to draw up a contract
einen Vertrag erneuern: to renew a contract
der stillschweigend geschlossene Vertrag: tacit agreement, implied contract
Vertragsbestimmungen einhalten: to conform to the conditions of a contract
der Vertragsentwurf: draft contract
die Vertragsstrafe: penalty

der **Vertragsteilnehmer**: partner (in a contract)
die **Vertragsverletzung**: infringement of a contract
der **Vertrauensschaden**: loss incurred from breach of contract
die **Vertrauenswerbung**: public relations
vertreiben: to sell, distribute
vertreten: to represent (a firm)
der **Vertreter**: representative or agent
die **Vertreterbefugnisse**: duties of an agent
der **Vertreterbezirk**: area of an agency
die **Vertreterprovision**: agent's commission
die **Vertretung**: agency
der **Vertrieb**: sale or distribution
der **Vertriebskostenplan**: forecast of marketing costs
der **Vertriebsleiter**: marketing manager
die **Vertriebsforschung**: marketing research
das **Vertriebsprogramm**: marketing plan
die **Verwaltungskosten**: administration costs
verwalten: to administer
verweigern: refuse
das **Verzeichnis**: list
verzollt: duty paid
die **Voll-Service Werbeagentur**: full service advertising
die **Vorauszahlung**: payment in advance/before dispatch
der **Vorbehalt**: reservation or restriction
vorführen: to demonstrate, to show
die **Vorführung**: demonstration (of an article)
vorgehen (gegen jemanden gerichtlich): to institute (legal proceedings against someone)
das **Vorkommnis**: event
vorlegen: to present (a bill, etc.)
vorschlagen: to suggest
die **Vorschrift**: rule, decree
VORSICHT! (auf Kisten): TAKE CARE! (on boxes)
die **Vorskizze (rohe)**: (rough) draft layout
das **geschäftsführende Vorstandsmitglied**: managing director

sich etwas vorstellen: to think of, to imagine
sich jemandem vorstellen: to introduce oneself to someone
der **Vorteil**: advantage
vorteilhaft: advantageous
den Vorteil ziehen (aus): to take advantage of something
der **Waggon**: (railway) truck
das **Warenausgangskonto**: account sales
der **Warenbestand**: stock, inventory
der **Warenempfänger**: consignee
die **Währung**: currency
das **Währungsrisiko**: exchange risks
die **Währungsschwankung**: exchange fluctuation
das **Warenhaus**: store or large shop
die **Warenprobe**: sample
die **Warenverkehrsbescheinigung**: movement certificate
die **Warenverteilung**: distribution of goods
das **Warenzeichen**: trade-mark
das **eingetragene Warenzeichen**: registered trade-mark
wasserdicht: watertight or waterproof
der **Wechsel**: bill of exchange (B/E)
einen Wechsel ziehen (auf jemanden): to draw a bill of exchange (on someone)
der **30-Tage Wechsel**: 30-day bill
die **Wellpappe**: corrugated paper
die **Werbeagentur**: advertising agency
der **Werbeanspruch (übertriebene)**: claim (sweeping)
die **Werbeaktion**: advertising campaign
der **Werbeblock**: advertising periods (T.V.)
die **Werbebotschaft**: advertising message
der **Werbebrief**: sales letter
die **Werbeerfolgskontrolle**: checking on advertising success, keying
der **Werbeetat**: advertising budget
der **genehmigte Werbeetat**: advertising appropriation or budget
der **Werbefachmann**: advertising expert or advertising man
der **Werbefeldzug**: advertising campaign
die **Werbeforschung**: advertising research
der **Werbefunk**: radio advertising

der Werbegemeinte: advertising target
die Werbekampagne: advertising campaign
die Werbekonzeption: advertising concept
die Werbekosten: advertising costs
der Werbekostenplan: advertising budget
der Werbeleiter: advertising manager
die Werbemassnahmen: advertising measures
das Werbemittel: advertising medium or media (general sense)
die Werbemittelforschung: media research
werben (er wirbt): advertise (he advertises)
der Werbeplan: advertising budget
das Werbeschild: sign board
die Werbesendung: advertising broadcast ('commercial' on radio or T.V.)
die Werbeszene: 'commercial' (T.V.)
der Werbeträger: advertising medium (specific), the means by which contact is made between the public and the general media; examples are newspapers, magazines, etc.
das Werbeziel: advertising target
die Werbung in Filmtheatern: cinema advertising
die Werbung in Verkehrsmitteln: advertising in public transport
die institutionelle Werbung: institutional advertising (prestige)
die Werbung um öffentliches Vertrauen: public relations
der Werbungstreibender: advertiser
ab Werk: ex-works
der Wertzoll: 'ad valorem' duty
der Wettbewerb: competition
der unlautere Wettbewerb: unfair competition
widerruflich: revocable
die Wirtschaftsinformation: economic information
der Wohnsitz: domicile
der Wortlaut: wording (terms of contract)

zahlbar bei Auftragserteilung: cash with order
zahlen: to pay
die Zahlung: payment
das Zahlenmaterial: data, figures
die Zahlung auf Ziel: payment on credit terms
Zahlung leisten: to make payment
die Zahlung bei Eingang der Waren: payment on receipt of goods
die Zahlungsbedingungen: conditions of payment
die Zahlungsfrist: term of payment (in time)
die Zahlungsmodalität: method of payment
der Zahlungstermin: day of payment or of maturity (B/E)
die Zahlungsüberweisung: remittance, bank transfer
das Zahlungsversprechen: promissary note
die Zahlungsweise: method of payment
das Zahlungsziel: date or time of payment
die Zeichnung: drawing
zeigen: to show, to display
der Zeilenpreis: price per line
auf unbestimmte Zeit: for an indefinite period
die Zeitpolice: 'floating', 'declaration' or 'open' policy
die Zeitschrift: magazine
die Zeitung: newspaper
der Zeitwechsel: time bill
zerbrechlich: fragile
zerlegen: dismantle/knock down (a piece of machinery)
der Zentraleinkauf: central buying
auf Ziel (Zahlung): on credit
gegen 3 Monate Ziel: against 3 months credit
die Zielgruppe: target group
der Zoll: customs duty
die Zollabfertigung: customs clearance
der Zollagent: customs agent
das Zollamt: customs office
Zoll einrichten: to clear customs
zollfrei: duty free
der Zollmakler: customs house broker
die Zollmaklergebühren: customs broker's fees
die Zollrückvergütung: repayment of duties paid or 'drawback'

das Zollsiegel: customs seal
die Zolltarifnummer: customs tariff number
der Zollverschluss: customs seal
das Zufallsverfahren: random sampling
der Zug: train
der durchgende Zug: through-train
zusammenfassen: to group or combine
zusammenstellen: to group or combine (various loads)

einwandfreier Zustand: perfect condition
die Zustellung: delivery
zuverlässig: safe or reliable
die Zweigniederlassung: subsidiary, branch (general term)
Zweites Deutsches Fernsehen (2.DF): second German T.V. Channel (national, commercial)
die Zwischenlandung: intermediate landing or stop-over

Vocabulary

to accept (an offer): annehmen
to accept: akzeptieren
account executive: der Kontaktor
'account group' (for advertising agency): die Kontaktgruppe
account sales: das Warenausgangskonto
acknowledgement: die Bestätigung
acknowledgement of receipt: die Empfangsbestätigung
to acquire the goodwill of a business: die Kundschaft übernehmen
actual figure: die Ist-Zahl
address list: die Adressenliste
adhesive label: der Aufkleber
'ad-hoc' survey: die 'ad-hoc' Survey
'ad valorem' duty: der Wertzoll
advantage: der Vorteil
advantageous: vorteilhaft
advantageous (offer): günstig (Angebot)
advertise (he advertises): werben (er wirbt)
advertisement: die Anzeige, das Inserat
advertisement pillar: die Anschlagsäule
advertisement space: der Anzeigenraum
advertiser: der Werbungstreibende
advertising block: das Anzeigenklischee
advertising broadcast ('commercial' on radio or T.V.): die Werbesendung
advertising budget: der Werbeetat, der Werbekostenplan *oder* der Werbeplan
advertising campaign: die Werbekampagne
advertising card: die Anzeigenpreisliste
advertising charge: die Insertionsgebühr
advertising campaign: der Werbefeldzug *oder* die Werbeaktion
advertising concept: die Werbekonzeption
advertising costs: die Werbekosten
advertising copy: das Anzeigenmaterial, der Anzeigeninhalt *oder* der Anzeigentext
advertising expert *or* **advertising man:** der Werbefachmann
advertising manager: der Werbeleiter
advertising measures: die Werbemassnahmen
advertising medium *or* **media (general sense):** das Werbemittel *oder* das Medium (pl. Medien, Media)
advertising medium (specific), the means by which contact is made between the public and the general media; examples are newspapers, magazines, etc.: der Werbeträger
advertising message: die Werbebotschaft
advertising periods (T.V.): der Werbeblock
to administer: verwalten
administration costs: die Verwaltungskosten
advertising, publicity: die Reklame
advertising copy: das Prospektmaterial
advertising in public transport: die Werbung in Verkehrsmitteln
advertising agency: die Werbeagentur
advertising appropriation *or* **budget:** der genehmigte Werbeetat
advertising rate: der Anzeigenpreis
advertising research: die Werbeforschung
advertising target: das Werbeziel *oder* der Werbegemeinte
advice: die Beratung
aeroplane: das Flugzeug
after-sales service: der Kundendienst
agency: die Vertretung, die Agentur
agency agreement: der Agenturvertrag
agency commission: die Agenturprovision
agent: der Agent, der Vertreter
agent (in legal sense): der Auftragnehmer
agent's commission: die Vertreterprovision
to agree (a price): vereinbaren (einen Preis)
archive materiel: das Archivmaterial
area agent: der Bezirksvertreter
air-cargo carrier: die Luftfrachtgesellschaft
air express service: der Luft-Expressdienst
airfreight: die Luftfracht
airline: die Flugverkehrsgesellschaft, die Luftverkehrsgesellschaft *oder* die Fluglinie

air parcel post: die Luftpaketpost
air/rail traffic: der FLEI-Verkehr (Flugzeug/Eisenbahnverkehr)
airway bill *or* **air waybill**: der Luftfrachtbrief
airway forwarding agent: der Luftfrachtspediteur
airway service office: das Luftfrachtkontor
by air: auf dem Luftweg
to allow, permit: erlauben
'all risks' insurance: die 'all risks' Versicherung
amount: der Bertrag, die Stückzahl, die Menge *oder* die Quantität
to appeal to (as advertisement to customer): ansprechen
applicable law: das massgebende Recht
to appoint: einsetzen, ernennen
arbitration: das Schiedsverfahren, der Schiedsspruch
arbitrator: der Schiedsrichter
area manager: der Gebietsleiter
area of an agency: der Vertreterbezirk
area sample: die regionale Marktuntersuchung
arrangement: die Gestaltung
to arrive (at a destination): eintreffen (in)
to arrive at a price, to calculate a price: einen Preis berechnen, kalkulieren
arrangement (of shop window, etc.): die Gestaltung
to ask for information: um Auskunft bitten
assessment: die Taxe
assortment, collection, range of goods: das Sortiment
assumption: die Annahme
average: der Durchschnitt
average, mean, median: der Mittelwert
average-analysis: die Durchschnittserhebung *oder* die Durchschnittsbestimmung
'average', damage (by sea): die Havarie
authoritative: massgebend
authority to collect (bills of exchange, etc.): die Inkassovollmacht

bad debts: verlorene Aussenstände
balance: der Restbetrag, der Saldo
balance payable: der Debitsaldo
balanced sample: die angepasste Stichprobe
bale: der Ballen
bank charges: die Bankspesen
(ordinary) bankruptcy: das Konkursverfahren (normale)
bankruptcy (reckless): der fahrlässige Bankrott
to go into bankruptcy, to go bankrupt: Konkurs machen, Bankrott machen
(bank) transfer: die (Bank) Überweisung, die Zahlungsüberweisung
basic price: der Grundpreis
basis: die Grundlage
to become due, to mature (a bill): fällig werden
best possible price: der äusserste Preis
bill: die Rechnung
bill of exchange (B/E): der Wechsel
(clean) Bill of Lading: das Konossement (rein)
billings (advertising): der Umsatz
not binding: unverbindlich
to bind oneself (by contract): sich binden, sich verpflichten
block (printing): die Stereotypieplatte
bonus: die Prämie
box: die Kiste
non-returnable box: die Einwegkiste
box or code numbers (for adverts): die Kennziffer
branch (legally dependent on parent company): die Filiale
branch (general term): die Zweigniederlassung
branch shop: die Filiale, der Filialbetrieb
brand advertising: die Markenwerbung
brand loyalty: die Markentreue
to break a contract: brechen (einen Vertrag)
broker: der Handelsmakler
brochure: die Broschüre
Brussels nomenclature: Brüsseler Zolltarif Schema
budgeted target: die Soll-Vorgabe
bulk-buying co-operative: die Grosseinkaufsgenossenschaft (G.E.G.)
bulk delivery: die Sammellieferung

VOCABULARY—ENGLISH/GERMAN

bulk goods: die Massengüter
bulk purchase: der Mengeneinkauf
bulky goods: das Sperrgut
burning: das Verbrennen
business expenses: die Geschäftsunkosten
businessman (trading on his own account): der Eigenhändler
business/trade secret: das Geschäftsgeheimnis
to do business with: ins Geschäft kommen
buyer: der Käufer
buying department: die Einkaufsabteilung
buying habit: die Einkaufsgewohnheit
buying motive: das Kaufmotiv
buying power: die Kaufkraft

to calculate: berechnen
to call at a port: einen Hafen anlaufen
to cancel a contract: aufheben (einen Vertrag)
capacity: der Rauminhalt
capacity to contract: die (Geschäfts) Vertragsfähigkeit
cardboard box: die Pappschachtel, der karton *oder* der Pappkarton
cardboard case: die Pappkiste
cardboard containers: die Kartonage
cardboard figure: das Pappmännchen
card index, address list: die Adressenkartei
cargo boat: das Frachtschiff
cargo: die Fracht, die Schiffsladung *oder* das Frachtgut
cargo hold: der Laderaum
to correct: berichtigen
carriage: die Beförderung
carriage forward: Frachtkosten per Nachnahme
carriage paid (C.P. or C.G.E. paid): frachtfrei
carrier: der Spediteur
carrying capacity: die Tragfähigkeit
cartage: das Rollgeld, die Rollspesen *oder* die Transportkosten
carton: der Karton
cash: der Geldbetrag
case under dispute: die Streitsache

cash against documents (C.A.D.): Kasse gegen Dokumente
cash and carry: (der) Cash-and-Carry Betrieb (C. & C. Betrieb)
to cash in (a coupon, etc.): einlösen
cash on delivery (C.O.D.): bei Lieferung zahlen
cash payment: die Barzahlung
cash transaction: das Bargeschäft
cash with order: zahlbar bei Auftragserteilung
catalogue: der Katalog
central buying: der Zentraleinkauf, der zentrale Einkauf
central buying organisation: die zentrale Einkaufsorganisation, die Einkaufszentrale
certificate of origin: das Ursprungszeugnis
certificate of shipment: die Versandbescheinigung, die Spediteurübernahmebescheinigung
certification: die Beglaubigung
to certify: beglaubigen
chain store: der Kettenladen
chain store business: das Kettenladenunternehmen
change: die Änderung
characteristic: die Eigenart
charge: die Gebühr
the charter party: der Chartervertrag
to check: prüfen
checked: geprüft
checking: das Prüfen
checking on advertising success, keying: die Werbeerfolgskontrolle
cheque: der Scheck
cinema: das Kino
cinema advertising: die Werbung in Filmtheatern
to circulate (catalogues, etc.): verbreiten, streuen, verteilen
circulation (of a newspaper, etc.): die Auflage (einer Zeitung u.s.w.)
claim (sweeping): der Werbeanspruch (übertriebene)
'classified' advertisement: die kleine Anzeige (Kleinanzeige)
clause: die Klausel
clearance, forwarding: die Abfertigung

client: der Kunde
clientele: der Kundenkreis
C.O.D.: gegen Nachnahme
C.O.D.: unter Nachnahme
collect (tax, etc.): erheben
collective transport: der Sammeltransport
collision at sea: der Schiffszusammenstoss
colour print: der Mehrfarbendruck
colour-T.V. advertisement: der farbige Fernsehspot
to combine (loads): zusammenstellen
combined offer: das kombinierte Angebot
'commercial' (T.V.): die Werbeszene
commercial agent: der Handelsvertreter
commercial invoice: die Handelsrechnung
commercial law: das Handelsrecht
commission: die Provision
commission agent: der Provisionsvertreter, der Kommissionär
to commit oneself: sich verpflichten
compensation: der Schadenersatz
to compete: konkurrieren
competition: die Konkurrenz, der Wettbewerb
competition (with prizes): das Preisausschreiben
unfair competition: unlauterer Wettbewerb
competitive: konkurrenzfähig
competitive price: der konkurrenzfähige Preis
competitor: der Konkurrent
comply with: nachkommen
composition type: der Schriftsatz
conciliation: die Schlichtung
to conduct business on one's own account: auf eigene Rechnung handeln
conditions of payment: die Zahlungsbedingungen
to confirm: bestätigen
confirmation: die Bestätigung
confirmed (as L/C.): bestätigt
to confirm in writing: schriftlich bestätigen
to conform or keep to a clause in a contract: einhalten (eine Vertragsbestimmung)

to conform to the conditions of a contract: Vertragsbestimmungen einhalten
connection: der Anschluss
to consign (goods): konsignieren
consignee: der Warenempfänger, der Empfänger
consignment note: der Frachtbrief
(rail) consignment note: der (Bahn) Frachtbrief
consignment stock: das Konsignationslager
consignor: der Absender
constriction: die Ausführung
consular invoice: die Konsulatfaktura
consumer: der Verbraucher
consumer buying habit: die Verbrauchergewohnheit
consumer panel: das Verbraucherpanel
consumer research: die Konsumforschung, die Verbraucherforschung
container: der Behälter, der Container
container depot: die Container-Anlage, das Container-Depot, der Behälterumschlagplatz *oder* der Container-Lagerplatz
container (dispatch) depot (with customs office): die Container-Abfertigungsanlage
container express train: der Container-Schnellzug
container groupage traffic: der Container-Sammelgutverkehr
container rail-ferry: das Eisenbahn-Container Schiff
container service: der Containerdienst
container terminal: das Container-Terminal
container traffic: der Behälterverkehr
container (transfer) depot: der Container-Umschlagplatz
container transport: der Container-Transport
container with doors at rear or both ends: der Endlader
container with side doors: Container mit Seitentüren
continuous survey: die Marktbeobachtung
the contract: der Vertrag
contract of carriage: der Speditionsvertrag

contract of carriage: der Frachtvertrag
contract of carriage: der Beförderungsvertrag
controlled sample: die charakteristische Marktuntersuchung
to convert (money): umrechnen
to convince oneself: sich überzeugen
co-operative buying association: die Einkaufsgenossenschaft
co-operative society: der Konsumverein
co-operative society: die Konsumgenossenschaft
copy (of B/L., etc.): die Ausfertigung
corrosion protection: der Korrosionsschutz
corrugated paper: die Wellpappe
C. & F. (cost and freight): Kosten und Fracht
cost of premises: die Raumkosten
cost of production: der Selbstkostenpreis
cost price: der Einstandspreis
costs: die Kosten (plur.)
counter display: die Ladentischauslage
coupon: der Coupon, der Gutschein
the court: das Gericht
court of arbitration: das Schiedsgericht
court of law: das Gericht
cover: der Deckel
coverage: die Reichweite, die Streuung
coverage: die Streubreite
covert advertising (editorials, etc.): die Schleicherwerbung
coverage costs: die Streukosten
crate: die Lattenkiste
creative division: die Gestaltungsgruppe
creative work: die Gestaltung
on credit terms (payment): auf Ziel (Zahlung)
credit balance: der Guthabensaldo
credit house: das Kredithaus
credit worthiness: die Kreditfähigkeit
cross section: der Querschnitt
cubic measure: das Kubikmass
currency: die Währung
customer: der Kunde
customer (potential): der Kunde (voraussichtlich, möglich)
longstanding customer: der Stammkunde
customer research: die Käuferforschung

customers: die Kundschaft, der Kundenkreis
customs: der Zoll
customs agent: der Zollagent
customs broker's fees: die Zollmaklergebühren
to clear customs: Zoll einrichten
customs clearance: die Zollabfertigung
customs duty: der Zoll
customs house broker: der Zollmakler
customs office: das Zollamt
customs seal: der Zollverschluss, das Zollsiegel
customs tariff number: die Zolltarifnummer

damage: der Schaden (pl. Schäden), die Beschädigung
30-day bill: der 30-Tage Wechsel
30 days net: 30 Tage netto
day of payment or of maturity (B/E): der Zahlungstermin
daily paper: die Tageszeitung
data: das Zahlenmaterial
date or time of payment: das Zahlungsziel
deadline: der Fristablauf, der Termin
dealer: der Händler
debt collecting: die Einziehung von Schulden
to decide: sich entscheiden
'declarations' policy: die laufende Police
decree: die Vorschrift
decry: verrufen
deduct (from payment): einbehalten, abziehen
defect: der Mangel, der Schaden
defective: fehlerhaft
deficient: fehlerhaft
to define: bestimmen
delay: die Verspätung
'del credere' agent: der Garantievertreter
'del credere' commission: die Delkredereprovision
delivery: die Zustellung, die Lieferung
delivery date: der Liefertermin
delivery note: der Lieferschein
delivery period: die Lieferfrist
delivery time: die Lieferfrist
to demand: verlangen

demand (for goods): die Nachfrage
to demonstrate: vorführen
demonstrate, to (an advantage): nachweisen (einen Vorteil)
demonstration (of an article): die Vorführung
department manager: der Abteilungsleiter
deposit: die Anzahlung
depth interview: das Tiefinterview
to describe: beschreiben
description(s): die Bezeichnung(-en)
design: die Ausführung, der Entwurf *oder* die Gestaltung
desk work: die Schreibtischarbeit
destruction: der Verderb
detail(s): die Angabe(n)
detrimental: nachteilig
direct method: die direkte Methode
direct dispatch: direkte Beförderung
direct mail advertising: die Postversandwerbung, die Direktwerbung
director: der Direktor
disadvantage: der Nachteil
disappearance: die Verschollenheit
to disclose: offenlegen
to discount: diskontieren
discount house: das Diskonthaus
discount: der Rabatt, der Skonto, der Nachlass
dismantle (a piece of machinery): zerlegen
to dismiss: entlassen
dismissal: die Kündigung
dispatch note: die Versandanzeige
display: die Gestaltung
to display: ausstellen
display area: die Ausstellungsfläche
display board: der Aufsteller
display material: das Display-Material
the dispute: der Streit
to distribute (sales): vertreiben, absetzen
distribute (catalogues, etc.): verbreiten, streuen *oder* verteilen
distribution (of goods): der Absatz und Vertrieb, die Warenverteilung
distribution area: das Verbreitungsgebiet
distribution channel: der Absatzweg
distributor: der Verteiler
to disturb: stören
dock: die Dockanlage, die Hafenanlagen

docker: der Dockarbeiter
dockside transfer charge: die Kai-Umschlaggebühr
documentary draft: die Dokumententratte
documentary letter of credit: das Dokumentenakkreditiv
documentation: die Unterlage
documents against acceptance (D/A): Dokumente gegen Wechselakzept
documents against payment (D/P): Dokumente gegen Zahlung
domicile: der Wohnsitz
door-to-door transport: der Haus-Haus Transport
draft (banking): die Tratte
(rough) draft layout: die Vorskizze (rohe)
to draw a bill of exchange (on someone): einen Wechsel ziehen (auf jemanden)
draft contract: der Vertragsentwurf
'drawback' (customs): die Zollrückvergütung
drawing: der Plan, die Zeichnung
to draw up a contract: einen Vertrag aufsetzen
driver-accompanied vehicle: das begleitete Fahrzeug
due: fällig
dues: die Abgaben (pl.)
durability: die Dauerhaftigkeit
duties of an agent: die Vertreterbefugnisse
duty free: zollfrei
duty paid: verzollt *oder* gesteuert
duty unpaid: unverzollt

economic information: die Wirtschaftsinformation
to effect (an insurance): abschliessen (eine Versicherung)
employer's profit: der Unternehmergewinn
to enclose (with letter, etc.): beifügen
to endorse: indossieren
to enter into an agreement: abschliessen (einen Vertrag)
enquiry (for goods): die Anfrage
enquiry (market research): die Umfrage, die Erhebung, die Enquete

VOCABULARY—ENGLISH/GERMAN 131

European Economic Community (E.E.C.): Europäische Wirtschaftsgemeinschaft (E.W.G.)
evaluation: die Auswertung
event: das Vorkommnis
to examine: prüfen
to exceed: überschreiten
exchange control: die Devisenkontrolle
exchange risk: das Währungsrisiko
exclusive agency: die Alleinvertretung
exclusive agent: der Alleinvertreter
exclusive right: das Alleinrecht
exclusive selling right: das Alleinverkaufsrecht
execution (carrying out): die Ausführung
execution of an order: die Auftragserledigung
expansion: die Expansion
expenditure: der Kostenaufwand
expenses: die Spesen
expert opinion: die Begutachtung
expiry of (a contract): der Ablauf (eines Vertrages)
export: die Ausfuhr
export department: die Exportabteilung
export licence: die Ausfuhrbewilligung
export manager: der Exportleiter
export market research: die Auslandsmarktforschung
export packing: die Exportverpackung
export packing case: die Exportkiste
export statistics: die Ausfuhrstatistiken
express air-freight: die Luft-Expressfracht
express goods: das Eilgut
expressly: ausdrücklich
express parcel service: das Expressgut
extension of time (granted to debtor, etc.): die Nachfristsetzung
ex-works: ab Werk
eye-catcher (advertising): der Blickfang

factory overheads: die Fertigungsgemeinkosten
fast goods train: der Eilgüterzug
faulty: fehlerhaft
in favour of: zu Gunsten
fee: die Gebühr
fee (flat): das Pauschalhonorar
fees: die Abgaben
ferry (-boat): die Fähre
ferry: das Fährschiff
ferry time: die Überseezeit
final art work: die Reinzeichnung
fibre-drum (for packing): die Fibertrommel
field work: die Feldarbeit
financial: finanziell
financial standing: die finanzielle Lage
firm offer: das Festangebot
firm price: der feste Preis
to fit: passen (jemanden)
fixed expenses: die Fixkosten
fixed salary: festes Gehalt
financial year: das Rechnungsjahr
'flat rate' policy: die Pauschalpolice
'floating' policy: die Zeitpolice, die laufende Police
fluctuations in price: die Preisschwankung
'force majeure': die höhere Gewalt
to have the force of law: rechtskräftig sein
forecast of marketing costs: der Vertriebskostenplan
forecast figure: die Sollzahl
forklift truck: der Gabelstapler
the form: das Formular
forwarding agent: der Spediteur
forwarding carrier: der Absenderspediteur
forwarding charges: die Versandspesen
forwarding instructions: die Versandvorschriften
forwarding instructions: die Versandanweisungen
fragile: zerbrechlich
free alongside ship (f.a.s.): frei Längsseite Schiff
franco (FCO) domicile: frei Haus
free on board (F.O.B.): frei an Bord, franko Bord, frei Schiff
free on rail (F.O.R.): frei Bahnwagen, frei Waggon
free on truck (F.O.T.): frei Güterwagen/Lastkraftwagen
F.P.A. Policy (free of particular average): Frei von Beschädigung ausser im Strandungsfall

F.P.A. Policy: die Versicherung ohne Particular Havarie
freight: die Fracht
freight: das Frachtgut
freight carrier: der Frachtführer
freight charges: die Frachtkosten
freight forward: Fracht gegen Nachnahme
frequency of insertion: die Anzeigenhäufigkeit
full load: die (volle) Ladung
full service advertising agency: die Voll-Service Werbeagentur

gain: der Nutzen, der Gewinn
gatekeeper: der Portier
gift: der Geschenkartikel
German Standards Institute (equivalent to B.S.I.): D.I.N. (Deutsches Institut für Normen)
German State Railway: die Deutsche Bundesbahn
general agent: der Generalvertreter
G.A. (general average): die grosse (gemeinschaftliche) Havarie
general cargo box container: der General Cargo Box Container
general cargo rates: allgemeine Frachtraten
general store: das Gemischtwarengeschäft, das Sortimentgeschäft
general overheads: die allgemeinen Unkosten
good selling line: der Verkaufsschlager
good standing: die Bonität
goods train: der Güterzug
goodwill of a business: der Goodwill, immaterieller Firmenwert
gross national product: das Bruttosozialprodukt
gross negligence: grobe Fahrlässigkeit
to group (various loads): zusammenstellen
group buying: der Sammeleinkauf
groupage transport: der Sammeltransport
group discussion: die Gruppendiskussion
groupage consignment: die Sammelladung
groupage traffic: der Sammelgutverkehr

guarantee: die Garantie, die Gewährleistung
to guarantee: garantieren, bürgen

handbill: das Flugblatt
to handle: handhaben
handling charges: die Verwaltungskosten
to hand over (B/L., etc.): aushändigen
haulage firm: das Transportunternehmen
haulier: der Transportunternehmer
head buyer: der Leiter, die Einkaufsabteilung *oder* der Einkaufschef
head office (of an agency, etc.): der Sitz (einer Vertretung)
hire purchase: der Abzahlungskauf
to hold in trust: (als) Fideikommiss besitzen, treuhänderisch verwalten
home market: heimischer Markt, der Inlandsmarkt
home market price: der Inlandspreis
household: der Haushalt, die Haushaltung
housekeeping diary: das Haushaltstagebuch

image: das Image
to imagine: sich (etwas) vorstellen
impact: der Stoss
impact (of an advertisement): die Stosskraft
impact resistance: die Stossfestigkeit
implied contract: der stillschweigend geschlossene Vertrag
import: die Einfuhr
to import: importieren
import duty: der Einfuhrzoll
importer: der Importeur
import licence: die Einfuhrlizenz, die Einfuhrbewilligung *oder* die Einfuhrgenehmigung
import quota: das Einfuhrkontingent
import statistics: die Einfuhrstatistiken
incentive: der Anreiz
income: das Einkommen
increase in price, extra charge: der Preisaufschlag
indefinite: unbestimmt
for an indefinite period: auf unbestimmte Zeit
to indemnify: entschädigen

independent: selbständig
index figure: die Indexzahl
indirect method: die indirekte Methode
to infringe a patent: ein Patent verletzen
infringement of a contract: die Vertragsverletzung
infringement of a patent: die Patentverletzung
inland transport: der Binnentransport
instalment: Rate, die Teilzahlungsrate, die Teilzahlung *oder* der Teilbetrag
to institute (legal proceedings against someone): vorgehen (gegen jemanden gerichtlich)
institutional advertising (Prestige): die institutionelle Werbung
insurance: die Versicherung
insurance agent: der Versicherungsagent
insurance broker: der Versicherungsmakler
insurance certificate: das Versicherungszertifikat
insurance company: die Versicherungsgesellschaft
insurance cover note: die Versicherungsdeckungsnote
insurance policy: die Versicherungspolice
insured: der Versicherte
insurer: der Versicherer
to be interested in something: sich für etwas interessieren
intermediate landing: die Zwischenlandung
international forwarding: die internationale Spedition
interview: die Befragung
interviewee: der Befragte
interviewer: der Befrager
intra E.E.C. tariff: der Binnentarif
to introduce oneself to someone: sich jemandem vorstellen
introduction: die Einleitung
inventory: der Warenbestand
irrevocable: unwiderruflich
item: der Posten, die Position

jet plane: das Düsenflugzeug
job: die Stellung

junk shop: der Kramladen, die Trödelbude
jurisdiction: der Gerichtsstand

to keep in store: auf Lager halten
to keep to (delivery date): einhalten
to knock down (machinery): zerlegen
knock: der Stoss (pl. Stösse)

labour costs: die Lohnkosten
large shop: das Warenhaus
LASH lighter aboard ship: LASH-Frachter (Schuten auf Seeschiff)
law, right: das Recht
law of equity: das Billigkeitsrecht
layout: das Layout, die Rohskizze
leaflet: das Flugblatt
legal: gesetzlich
legislation: die Gesetzgebung
letter of credit: das Akkreditiv
to levy (tax, etc.): erheben
liable to pay damages: schadenersatzpflichtig
to be held liable: haften
liability: die Haftung
to liberalise: liberalisieren
lid: der Deckel
life: die Lebensdauer
limited company: die Aktiengesellschaft (A.G.)
limited company: Gesellschaft mit beschränkter Haftung (G.m.b.H./ GMBH.)
list: das Verzeichnis
'literature': die Unterlage
load: die Last
to load: laden, verladen
loading: die Verladung
local agent: der Platzvertreter
to look for: suchen
long distance road haulage: der Güterfernverkehr
long distance haulier: der Fernspediteur
lorry: der Lastkraftwagen (LKW)
lorry trailer: der Kraftfahrzeuganhänger
loss: der Verlust
loss (being mislaid): das Abhandenkommen
loss incurred from breach of contract: der Vertrauensschaden

lower a price: einen Preis herabsetzen, ermässigen, senken
lump-sum freight: die Pauschalfracht

magazine: die Zeitschrift, das Magazin
magazine library: der Lesezirkel
mail order business: das Versandgeschäft, das Versandhaus
manager: der Geschäftsführer
manager or head clerk (with power to sign binding contracts and to represent the firm in a court of law): der Prokurist
managing director: der Betriebsführer, der Geschäftsführer *oder* das geschäftsführende Vorstandsmitglied
manifest: das Ladeverzeichnis
manufacturer's agent: der Handelsvertreter
(gross) margin: die Handelsspanne
market: der Markt
marketability: die Absatzfähigkeit
market analysis: die Marktanalyse
market conditions: die Konjunktur
market research: die Marktforschung
market researcher: der Marktforscher
market survey: die Marktanalyse
market survey: die Marktuntersuchung
marketing: das Marketing, der Absatz, der Vertrieb, die Absatzwirtschaft
marketing area: das Absatzgebiet
marketing manager: der Vertriebsleiter
marketing method: die Absatzmethode
marketing plan: das Vertriebsprogramm
marketing plan: die Absatzprognose, der Absatzplan
marketing research: die Vertriebsforschung, die Absatzforschung
marketing statistic: die Absatzstatistik
marketing territory: das Absatzgebiet
marking (on a package, etc.): die Markierung
mark-up: der Aufschlag, der Rohgwinnaufschlag
mass media: die Massen-Medien
material: das Material
material costs: die Materialkosten
mate's receipt: der Kai-Empfangsschein
maturity (of bill): die Fälligkeit

at maturity: bei Fälligkeit
manager: der Manager
measure: das Mass
media chosen for advertising campaign: der Streuweg
media expenditure: die Streukosten
media planning: die Streuung
media planning division: die Streuungsgruppe
media research: die Mediaforschung, die Werbemittelforschung
media schedule: die Streuung
media strategy: die Streuplanung
to meet: nachkommen
to meet the deadline: die Frist einhalten
merchandising: die Verkaufsunterstützung
merchandising: das Merchandising
method of dispatch: die Versandart
method of packing: die Verpackungsart
method of payment: die Zahlungsmodalität, die Zahlungsweise
method of transport: die Beförderungsart
millimeter height (of an advertisement) (c.f. column-inch): die Millimeterhöhe
minimum income: das Mindesteinkommen
monthly account: die Monatsberechnung
monthly settlement: der Monatsabschluss
against 3 months credit: gegen 3 Monate Ziel
motivational research: die Motivforschung
motorised: motorisiert
movement certificate: die Warenverkehrsbescheinigung

nailing: die Vernagelung
to name: benennen
nature (of goods): die Beschaffenheit
to need: benötigen, brauchen
negligence: die Fahrlässigkeit
negotiable: übertragbar
nett cost: der Selbstkostenpreis
nett profit: der Reinverdienst
newspaper: die Zeitung
non-returnable packing: Verpackung zum Wegwerfen
number of columns: die Spaltenzahl

offer: die Offerte, das Angebot
offer of limited duration: das befristete Angebot
offer subject to alteration: das freibleibende Angebot
offer without obligation (not binding): das unverbindliche Angebot
office expenses: die Bürounkosten
office supplies: der Bürobedarf
to open (an account, a letter of credit): eröffnen
open account: offene Rechnung, laufende Rechnung
to have an open account: in laufender Rechnung stehen
open policy: die laufende Police
to open a shop/business: eröffnen (ein Geschäft)
order(s): die Bestellung, der Auftrag (Aufträge)
to order: bestellen
order form: das Auftragsformular, der Bestellschein, der Bestellzettel
outlet: das Absatzgebiet
outstanding debt: der Aussenstand
overheads: die Geschäftsunkosten, die Betriebsunkosten
overseas agent: der Auslandsvertreter
own brand: die Hausmarke
open-top container: offener Container

to pack: verpacken, einpacken
packing: die Verpackung
packing charged extra: Verpackung besonders berechnet
inner packing: die innere Verpackung
page: die Seite
page rate: der Seitenpreis
pallet: die Palette
parcel: das Paket
by parcel post: als Paket schicken
partial statistical 'universe': die Teilmasse
particular(s): die Angabe(n)
particular average: die kleine Havarie
partner (in a contract): der Vertragsteilnehmer
part-page: die Teilseite, der Seitenteil
patent right: das Patentrecht
patented: gesetzlich geschützt

to pay (a debt): begleichen
to pay: zahlen
to pay cash: barzahlen
payment: die Zahlung
lump sum payment: die Pauschalzahlung
to make payment: Zahlung leisten
payment before dispatch: die Vorauszahlung
payment by instalments: die Ratenzahlung
payment in advance: die Vorauszahlung
to pay into an account: auf ein Konto einzahlen
payment on credit terms: Zahlung auf Ziel
payment on receipt of goods: Zahlung bei Eingang der Waren
penalty: die Vertragsstrafe
penalty clause: die Strafklausel
percentage: der Prozentanteil
performance: die Vorführung
perfect condition: einwandfreier Zustand
period of notice: die Kündigungsfrist
period of validity: die Gültigkeitsdauer
personnel manager: der Personaldirektor
piece goods: das Stückgut
place of delivery: der Erfüllungsort
plastic: der Kunststoff
plastic foil: die Kunststoff-Folie
to play an important part: eine bedeutende Rolle spielen
to place an order: einen Auftrag erteilen, einen Auftrag aufgeben
plywood case: die Sperrholzkiste
policy: die Police
'open' policy: die Generalpolice
poll (market research): die Enquete, die Erhebung, die Umfrage
population: die Bevölkerung
port dues: die Hafengebühren
port of departure: der Abgangshafen
port of embarkation: der Verschiffungshafen
position (job): die Stellung
position (physical): die Lage
position (of an advertisement on page): der Platz
possible: eventuell
presentation (of advertisement, etc.): die Gestaltung

post office: die Post
postal charges: die Postgebühren
postal cheque: der Postscheck
postal service: die Post
poster: das Plakat
poster column: die Litfasssäule
poster- or outdoor advertising: die Anschlagwerbung
premium: die Prämie
to present (a bill, etc.): präsentieren, vorlegen
pressure of costs: der Kostendruck
prestige advertising: die Prestigewerbung
price: der Preis
price control: die Preisüberwachung
price increase: die Preiserhöhung
lowest price: der äusserste Preis, der niedrigste Preis
price per line: der Zeilenpreis
a reasonable price: ein mässiger Preis
price list: die Preisliste
price list: das Preisverzeichnis
price range: die Preislage, die Preisskala
price reduction: der Preisnachlass, die Preisermässigung
regular price: der Normalpreis
price regulation: die Preisverordnung
primary material: die Primärdaten, das Primärmaterial
principal (e.g. client for whom a research company works): der Auftraggeber
principal (e.g. in a contract): der Unternehmer
prejudicial: nachteilig
principal (in legal sense): der Auftraggeber
(print or press) advertising: die Anzeigenwerbung
printing block: der Klischeefuss
production costs: die Gestehungskosten
product research: die Produktforschung
production division: die Produktionsgruppe
production manager: der Produktionsleiter
profit: der Nutzen, der Gewinn
profit margin: die Gewinnspanne, die Handelsspanne
proforma invoice: die Proformarechnung

programme magazine: die Programmzeitschrift
promissary note: Zahlungsversprechen
prompt payment: die Promptzahlung
proof: der Beweis
proof (sheet): der Probeabzug
prospectus: der Prospekt
to protect: schützen
protected by law (patented): gesetzlich geschützt
protection: der Schutz
to prove (an advantage): nachweisen (einen Vorteil)
public relations: die Vertrauenswerbung, die Werbung um öffentliches Vertrauen
public relations division: die Public-Relations-Gruppe
public relations work: die Offentlichkeitsarbeit
'pull' (printing): der Probeabzug
purchasing group: der Einkaufsverband
purchase price: der Einkaufspreis

quality: die Qualität
quantity: die Stückzahl, die Menge, die Quantität
quantity discount: der Mengenrabatt
quantity rebate: der Mengennachlass, der Mal-Nachlass
quantity reduction: der Mengennachlass, der Mal-Nachlass
quarter (three months): das Quartal
quarterly bill: die Quartalsrechnung
quarterly credit: der vierteljährliche Rechnungsabschluss
quarterly payment: die Quartalszahlung
quarterly statement of account: die Quartalsabrechnung
quay: der Kai
questionnaire: der Fragebogen
quota: das Kontingent, die Quote
quota samples: die Stichprobenanalyse
quota sampling: das Quotenverfahren
quotation: das Angebot
to quote: anbieten
to quote prices: Preise angeben

rack: das Gestell
radio: der Rundfunk

radio advertising: der Werbefunk, die Hörfunkwerbung
radio 'commercial': der Funkspot
radio script: der Funktext
rail-ferry container wagon: der Eisenbahnfähre-Sammelwaggon
railway transport: die Eisenbahnbeförderung
railway truck: der Waggon
to raise a price: einen Preis erhöhen, heraufsetzen, steigern
random sampling: das Randomverfahren, das Zufallsverfahren
random test: die Stichprobe
rate of commission: der Provisionssatz
rate of exchange: der Kursstand
readership: die Leserschaft
reading-circle: der Lesezirkel
rear door: die Hecktür
rebate: der Rabatt (pl. Rabatte), der Skonto, der Nachlass (pl. N'lässe)
recall test: der Erinnerungstest
receipt: die Quittung
to receipt an invoice: quittieren (eine Rechnung)
receipt of an order: der Auftragseingang
reception: der Empfang
recipient: der Empfänger
records: die Archivalien, das Archivmaterial
to rectify: berichtigen
to reduce a price: einen Preis ermässigen, herabsetzen, senken
reference book: das Nachschlagebuch
to refuse: ablehnen, verweigern
refrigerated container: der Kühl-Container
registered packet: das Einschreibepäckchen
registered parcel: das Einschreibepaket
registered trade-mark: das eingetragene Warenzeichen
reliable: zuverlässig
to reload: umladen
remittance: die Zahlungsüberweisung
remuneration: das Entgelt, die Entlohnung
to renew a contract: einen Vertrag erneuern
renewal: die Erneuerung

repayment of duties paid: die Zollrückvergütung
to represent (a firm): vertreten (eine Firma)
representative: der Vertreter
to require: brauchen
requirements: der Bedarf
to meet with the requirements: den Anforderungen entsprechen
research: die Forschung
qualitative research: die qualitative Forschung
quantitative research: die quantitative Forschung
reservation of proprietary right: der Eigentumsvorbehalt
reservation: die Einschränkung
restriction: die Einschränkung
retail cash and carry store: der Verbrauchermarkt
retailer: der Einzelhändler
retail price: der Einzelhandelspreis
retail shop: das Einzelhandelsgeschäft
in return for: als Gegenleistung
return service: die Gegenleistung
revocable: widerruflich
(right of) ownership: das Eigentumsrecht
risk: das Risiko
road haulage: der Strassengüterverkehr
roll-on/roll-off ferry ship: der Ro-Ro Frachter
room (space): der Raum
rule: die Vorschrift

safe: zuverlässig
safeguard: die Schutzvorrichtung
sales area: die Verkaufsfläche
salary: das Gehalt
salaries: die Personalkosten
sales: der Absatz, der Vertrieb, der Verkauf
sales budget: der Verkaufsplan
sales contract: der Verkaufsvertrag
sales engineer: der Verkaufsingenieur
sales forecast: die Verkaufsvoraussage, die Verkaufsprognose
sales figure: die Absatzziffer, der Umsatz
sales letter: der Werbebrief
salesman: der Verkäufer

sales management: die Verkaufsleitung
sales manager: der Verkaufsleiter
sales personnel: das Verkaufspersonal
sales promotion: die Verkaufsförderung
sales team: das Verkaufsteam
sales territory: das Absatzgebiet
sample: die Warenprobe, das Muster, die Probe
sample (Market Research): die Stichprobe
sample (registered design): das Gebrauchsmuster
biased sample: die einseitig betonte Stichprobe
representative sample: der repräsentative Querschnitt, die repräsentative Stichprobe
sample survey: die Stichprobenerhebung
quota sampling: das Quota-Sampling
screen: die Leinwand
seafreight rate: die Seefrachtrate
seal (usually of lead): die Plombe
sealed: plombiert
seasonal index: der Saisonindex
seaworthy: seefrachtmässig, seetüchtig
secondary material: das Sekundärmaterial
self-service shop: der Selbstbedienungsladen (S.B.-Laden)
self-service store: das Selbstbedienungswarenhaus
to sell: vertreiben, absetzen
to send: schicken
to send by rail: mit der Bahn schicken
service: die Dienstleistung
service agreement: der Dienstvertrag
service costs: die Dienstleistungskosten
service life: die Lebensdauer
to settle (business): erledigen
to settle a dispute by arbitration: einen Streit durch Schiedsspruch erledigen
shed: der Schuppen
sheet (of paper): der Bogen
to ship: befördern
shipping company: die Reederei, die Schiffahrtsgesellschaft
shipping: die Verschiffung
shipping document: das Transportdokument
shipping documents: die Versandpapiere
shipment: die Verschiffung
shipowner has the right to decide whether the goods are to be charged by volume or weight: 'in Schiffswahl'
shipper (shipping company): die Reederei
shipwreck: die Strandung
in case of shipwreck: im Strandungsfall
shop: der Laden
shop window: das Schaufenster
to show: zeigen, vorführen
showcase: der Ausstellkasten
showroom: der Ausstellungsraum
show window: das Auslagefenster
to sign a contract: abschliessen (Vertrag)
sign board: das Werbeschild
sight or demand draft or bill: die Sichttratte
sight or demand draft (D.D.): der Sichtwechsel
single policy: die Einzelpolice
sinking: das Versenken
situation: die Lage
sketch: die Skizze
skill in selling: die Verkaufsgewandtheit
slogan: das Schlagwort
society magazine: die Gesellschaftszeitschrift
sole agent: der Generalvertreter
solvency: die Bonität
source: die Quelle
source of information: die Informationsquelle
space schedule: der Streuplan
space charges (advertising): die Streukosten
space (physical): der Raum
special container vehicle: das Container-Spezialfahrzeug
special offer: das Sonderangebot
special offer: das preisgünstige Angebot
specialist: der Fachkaufmann
specialist periodical: das Fachblatt, die Fachzeitschrift
specialist shop: das Spezialgeschäft, das Fachgeschäft
specific duty: der Stückzoll
specific duty (based on quantity): der Mengenzoll
specific duty (based on weight): der Gewichtszoll

to specify: benennen (p.p. benannt)
spot, T.V.-colour: der farbige Fernsehspot
stand: der Ständer
standard price (price recommended by manufacturer but which trade is not obliged to adopt): der Richtpreis
standard size: das Standardformat
standard specification: die Normbezeichnung
standard steel container: der standard Stahl-Container
standing (status): die Lage
statement: der Kontoauszug
statistic: die Statistik
status: die Lage
steel bands (for securing a case): die Stahlbandverschnürung
'stereo' (block): die Stereotypieplatte
stock audit: die Lagerbestandsaufnahme
stock: der Warenbestand
stock turnover: der Lagerumsatz
stop over: die Zwischenlandung
storage: die Lagerung, die Lagerhaltung
storage charges: die Lagergebühren
storage costs: die Lagergebühren
store: das Lager
store: das Warenhaus
stranding: die Strandung
strike: der Streik
sub-agent: der Untervertreter
to submit an offer/a quotation: ein Preisangebot machen
subsidiary (general term): die Zweigniederlassung
subsidiary company (legally independent): die Tochtergesellschaft
to sue for damages: Schadenersatzklage erheben
to suffer (damage or loss): erleiden (Schaden)
to suggest: vorschlagen
to suit: passen (jemanden)
Sunday paper: die Sonntagszeitung
supermarket: der Supermarkt
supplier: der Lieferant
supply: die Lieferung
supply (as in supply and demand): das Angebot
to supply: liefern

survey: die Enquete, die Erhebung, die Umfrage
Swiss State Railway: die Schweizer Bundesbahn (S.B.B.)
synthetic varnish: der Kunststoff-Lack

T.A.T. (Thematical Apperceptional Test): der projektive Test
tacit agreement: der stillschweigend geschlossene Vertrag
to take advantage of something: den Vorteil ziehen (aus)
TAKE CARE! (on boxes): VORSICHT! (auf Kisten)
to take off a list: von einer Liste streichen
to take on (an agency): übernehmen (eine Vertretung)
to take (goods) on consignment: in Konsignation nehmen (Waren)
to take advantage of an opportunity: eine günstige Gelegenheit benutzen
to take out (insurance policy): erwerben (Versicherungspolice)
to take someone to court: gerichtlich gegen jemanden vorgehen
tare (weight): die Tara (Gewicht)
target group: die Zielgruppe
tariff classification: die Tarifeinordnung
tarred paper: das Teerpapier
tax: die Gebühr
tax relief: die Steuererleichterung
team of colleagues: der Mitarbeiterstab
telephone box: die Telefonzelle
telephone exchange: die Telefonzentrale
tendency: die Tendenz
technical sales representative: der technische Verkäufer
to terminate (a contract): beenden (ein Vertragsverhältnis)
terms of delivery: die Lieferbedingungen
terms of payment: das Zahlungsziel
term of payment (in time, not method): die Zahlungsfrist
to test: prüfen
test market: der Testmarkt
technical costs: die Gestaltungskosten
to think of: sich (etwas) vorstellen
to think over: überlegen

third party: der Dritte
'this side up': 'oben'
'through' bill of lading: das Durchkonnossement
through-container-transport: durchgehender Container-Transport
through pallet service: durchgehend pallettisierter Service
through rate: der Durchgangstarif
through railway-wagon: der Durchgangswagen
through-train: der durchgehende Zug
time bill: der Zeitwechsel
time limit (for payment, etc.): die Frist
time of delivery: die Lieferzeit
topical illustrated magazine: die aktuelle Illustrierte
total amount: der Rechnungsbetrag
total value: der Gesamtwert
tractor: der Traktor
tractor-drawn: motorisiert
to trade: handeln
trade directory: das Handelsadressbuch
trade-in: die Inzahlungnahme
trade journal: das Fachblatt, die Fachzeitschrift
trader: der Händler
tradesman: der Händler
trade-mark: das Warenzeichen
trading year: das Geschäftsjahr
trailer: der Trailer
trailor-tractor unit: der Lastzug
train: der Zug
train ferry: das Fährschiff
train ferry wagon: der Fährboot-Waggon
training: die Ausbildung, die Schulung
to transfer: übertragen
transfer of ownership: die Eigentumsübertragung
transferable: übertragbar
transit: die Durchfahrt, die Durchfuhr
transition period: die Übergangszeit
to transmit: übertragen
transparency: das Diapositiv
to transfer (goods): umladen
to transport: befördern
transport costs: die Transportkosten
travelling allowance: das Reisegeld
travelling expenses: die Reisekosten, die Reisespesen

trend: der Trend
trial period: die Probezeit
on trial: zur Prüfung
tropical protection: der Klimaschutz
turnover: der Umsatz
T.V. advertising: die Fernsehwerbung, die T.V.-Werbung
1st T.V. channel (regional, commercial): A.R.D. (Arbeitsgemeinschaft der Rundfunkgesellschaften Deutschlands)
second German T.V. Channel (national, commercial): Zweites Deutsches Fernsehen (2.DF)
Third T.V. channel (regional, non-commercial): Drittes (III.) Programm

unconfirmed: unbestätigt
underwriter: der Versicherer
unethical: sittenwidrig
unethical method: die unsaubere Methode
unit load: die Ladeeinheit
'universe' (population): die Gesamtmasse
unit load: die Einheitsladung
to unload: entladen
to unload a ship: löschen
to unpack: auspacken

valid: gültig
value added tax (V.A.T.): die Mehrwertsteuer (M.W.St.)
valuation: die Taxe
variable costs: variable Kosten
vehicle: das Fahrzeug
vibrations: die Schwingungen
volume: der Rauminhalt
voluntary chain (of shops): die freiwillige Kette
voucher (for collecting): der Gutschein, der Sammelgutschein
to vouch for: bürgen

wage: das Gehalt
wages: die Personalkosten
wall poster: der Maueranschlag
W.P.A. Policy (with particular average): Frei von Beschädigung wenn unter 3%
W.P.A. Policy: die Versicherung mit Havarie

warranty: die Gewährleistung
ex-warehouse: ab Lager
warning (unconditional request for performance): die Inverzugsetzung
waterproof: wasserdicht
watertight: wasserdicht
Way Bill: der Frachtbrief
weight (net, gross): das Gewicht (netto, brutto)
wholesaler: der Grosshändler
wildcat strike: der wilde Streik
to withdraw (from a list): streichen (von einer Liste)
without notice: fristlos
wooden box: die hölzerne Kiste
wooden crate: der Holzverschlag
wood-fibre box: die Holzfaserkiste
wording (terms of contract): der Wortlaut
works manager: der Fabrikleiter, der Betriebsleiter, der Betriebsführer
workmanship: die Ausführung
wrapping: die Verpackung

Bibliography

London Chamber of Commerce with the co-operation of the Hamburg Chamber of Commerce. *Federal Republic of Germany.*
HANS O. RASCHE. *Marketing aber mit System.* I. H. Sauer-Verlag.
P. SPILLARD. *Praktische Verkaufsförderung,* translated from the English by Werner Popp. Verlag Moderne Industrie.
HANS-GEORG LETTAU. *Marketing in der täglichen Praxis.* Econ Verlag.
This is Your German Market. Axel Springer Publishing Group.
DIPLOM-VOLKSWIRT GERHARDT HILDEBRAND. *Deutsch für Kaufleute.* Visaphone G.m.b.H.
JOSEPH HARVARD. *English-German Bilingual Guide to Business and Professional Correspondence.* Pergamon Press.
GUNTER WADUSCHAT. *Exportleiter Handbuch.* Verlag Moderne Industrie.
CLIVE M. SCHMITTHOF. *The Export Trade.* Stevens & Sons Ltd.
HENRY DESCHAMPNEUFS. *Marketing in the Common Market.* Pan Books, London.
British Embassy in Bonn. *Seeking and Working with a Commercial Agent in the Federal Republic of Germany.*
Praktische Hinweise für die Vertretung ausländischer Firmen. Albert Limbach Verlag, Braunschweig.
British Embassy in Bonn. *How to Advertise Goods of United Kingdom Manufacturers in Western Germany.*
Selling Consumer Goods to Western Germany. The British National Export Council (B.N.E.C.), London.
HEINZ GOLDMANN. *Wie man Kunden gewinnt.* Verlag W. Girardet, Essen.
DR JULIUS GREIFZU. *Handbuch des Kaufmanns.* Verlag Ullstein.